TRAINING GUIDE

Complete **WordPress** Training at your
fingertips to accelerate your success!

Table of Content

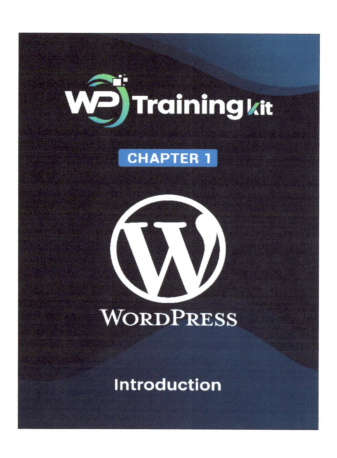

WordPress is an Open Source software system used by millions of people around the world to create beautiful websites and blogs. It is completely customizable by the use of themes and plugins.

Thanks to the great community of contributors and the constant development, WordPress has become a content management system that provides you with tons of features to build and manage your website.

You can use the application to build any type of website: from a small personal blog or business website to fully-featured eCommerce online store or gallery/portfolio website, the possibilities are endless. WordPress is the ideal solution to build your online presence, whether you are a newcomer or you already have some technical experience. As you have a great number of plugins to extend the functionality of your website, with no coding required you can create a professional website in just a few easy steps.

And that's exactly what we are going to discuss in this training guide. In this guide, we will provide you with detailed information and instructions on how you can use WordPress to build your own website with ease. We will cover different topics like WordPress installation, plugin and theme management, and usability. Also, you will learn how to extend the functionality of your WordPress website and provide your visitors with feature-rich experience.

So let's get started...

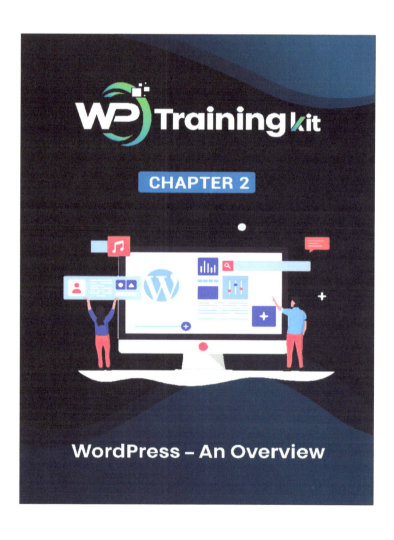

WordPress is one of the most widely-used blogging platforms available. WordPress is a factory that makes webpages is a core analogy designed to clarify what WordPress is and does. It stores the content that allows you to create & publish webpages only requiring a domain and a hosting site to work. Let's unveil it in detail…

2.1 What is WordPress?

WordPress is a Content Management System (CMS), which is open source and was created to manage blogs. WordPress allows you to easily create and manage your blogs and websites content without coding and it can be used to create a fully operational website.

Today, WordPress is the largest self-hosted blogging tool in the world being used by millions of websites. The best thing about WordPress is that it is an Open Source project which can be used by anyone over the web which means you can use it for anything be it your personal diary, your travel accounts or your views on any subject for that matter. WordPress is an excellent platform for building a variety of websites. Besides building a blogging site, WordPress can be used to build an e-commerce website, portfolio sites, business websites, new sites, and more. Famous WordPress websites include TechCrunch, Mashable, The New York Times's blog, etc.

Some of the features offered by WordPress are private and password protected WordPress posts and pages, easy importing, WordPress installation and upgrades, a full WordPress theme and plugin system, multiple authors, spam protection and intelligent text formatting. So, 'WordPress is only limited by your imagination'.

With its intuitive interface, ease of use and the great number of free and paid themes and plugins, WordPress is the preferred choice to build a professional website. All WordPress features are fully supported on all our WordPress hosting plans, so you can get started in no time and create your next successful online project.

2.2 What is Content Management System?

A content management system (CMS) is an application used to create and manage digital content. Content is what makes any organization stand out from the crowd, content must be regular and well organized in order to maintain any branding possible thus rather than doing it manually CMSes are used for enterprise content management (ECM) and web content management (WCM).

An ECM is used for the collaboration in any workplace by integrating document management, digital asset management and records retention functionalities, and providing end users with role-based access to the organization's digital assets. While WCM facilitates collaborative authoring for websites. It is easy to say that WCM is a more public content management tool whereas the ECM is totally built for more confidential contents to be kept secured within the organization.

2.3 How does WordPress work?

WordPress, like any other WCM system, is dynamically driven through the use of a database with multiple tables storing all the content information and the information required to specify the website structure. You must have the ability to create and utilize a database to use WordPress.

After learning about WordPress the first thing that comes to our mind is that where to use it? What kind of website can I create using WordPress? So let's move on to the section straight away.

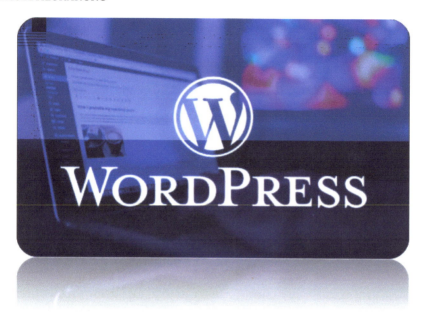

When launched, WordPress was nothing but a typographic improvement, but as time passed and the community got stronger and WordPress was developed by contributors from all over the world, now WordPress is a robust system that can be used to create and manage any kind of website to keep it short. To showcase some examples let's look into the various implementations of WordPress already developed.

- **E-commerce Websites:** WordPress is really great for E-Commerce websites because of its robust structure and ability to categorize contents. With the proper theme chosen to create an E-commerce website is considered to be one of the best options available.
- **Educational/Library Websites:** One of the most important features of WordPress is to manage and categorize documents or other assets, though not self-sustaining WordPress is good enough to create and run a Library Website. Using DMS implementation as well as WordPress one can surely develop Library Websites.
- **Personal Websites:** Whether it's a small website

containing your portfolio or a daily blog. WordPress is undoubtedly one of the best platforms to showcase your talent as it has dedicated sections for the contents and overall easy experience.

2.4 Features of WordPress

WordPress is considered to be the most popular content management system due to its characteristics:

- The most important features of WordPress are that you can create a dynamic website without any programming and design knowledge
- WordPress is theme based which provides you options for various open source and premium design themes, which can be integrated easily without any designing knowledge
- Plugins extend the functionality of WordPress, which can be used to add new required modules
- WordPress sites are search engine optimization (SEO) friendly, it means sites built in WordPress can be easily

optimized for search engine listings

- WordPress is Multilingual, which allow users to translate content in their language
- WordPress has inbuilt Media Management System which is used to manage images, music, documents, etc. and can be used with text content

2.5 The Benefits of Using WordPress

Here are just the top 5 benefits of using WordPress:

- **The software is free!** How many times have you been given something for free that is fully functional and ready to use? And if you want to upscale your site a little with premium themes and plugins, you're still going to save tons of money over what you would pay for a custom designed site.
- **It's easy to use.** Seriously. If you can send an email, use Microsoft Word, or set up a Facebook account, then you can use WordPress. In other words, if you've already used a computer, chances are you are already skilled enough for the WordPress basics. And even better, it's hard to mess it up. You can easily add and delete pages and posts without accidentally messing up the overall design of your site.
- **You are in control.** Owning your own site, and being able to make changes to it yourself, is the ultimate in online freedom. You don't have to rely on an expensive web designer to make changes or fix a tiny error for you whenever they can squeeze you in. You're in control of your site—and your wallet.
- **WordPress has a search engine (SEO) advantages.** Search engines love sites that are easy to index (WordPress is) and that have frequently updated content. That's where blogging comes in to play so nicely. Just by running your business or personal site and communicating with your readers in a way that's

natural to you, you'll be producing fresh, relevant content the search engines can't wait to get ahold of.

- **There's a HUGE support community.** WordPress isn't just software, it has become a community. Some might even say a movement. In fact, WordCamps (1-3 day training sessions) have sprung up from grassroots efforts. They are informal, community-organized events put together by other WordPress users just like you. You'll meet people of all backgrounds, ages, and nationalities at WordCamps. Plus, there are thousands of people and hundreds of resource and tutorial sites set up just to help you with your WordPress site.

2.6 WordPress.com vs. WordPress.org

The one major difference between WordPress.com and WordPress.org is who's actually hosting your website. With WordPress.org, YOU host your own blog or website. WordPress.org is where you'll find the free WordPress software that you can download and install on your own web server. Getting your WordPress site set up involves purchasing a domain name, buying a hosting plan and then installing WordPress on your server. Most hosting companies provide instructions or services to install WordPress for you.

WordPress.com, on the other hand, takes care of all of the hostings for you. You don't have to download software, pay for hosting, or manage a web server.

2.6.1 Pros and Cons of WordPress.com vs. WordPress.org

Both WordPress.org and WordPress.com have pros and cons, depending on your needs. If you're not interested in paying for your own hosting, managing your own web server or paying someone else to handle that for you, you'll probably want to use WordPress.com. It's free and easy to set up and you have lots of options for customizing your site. A few of the cons of using WordPress.com include that your domain will, by default, include

"WordPress.com."

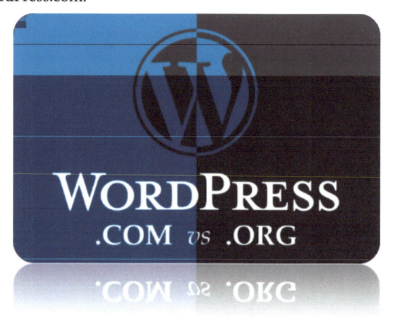

You also can't upload any custom themes, plugins or modify the PHP code behind your site. While WordPress.com is free to set up, they do offer several premium upgrades, including domain name registration (if you don't want WordPress.com in your domain name), the ability to upload videos and the option to use their premium themes.

Using the downloaded version of WordPress from WordPress.org opens up more control and flexibility for your WordPress site, but it also means more responsibility. Using a self-hosted version of WordPress means you can use your own domain name, upload and install themes and plugins, edit the code behind your site and have access to your site's database (or files). Most of the showcase sites you see on the WordPress site showcase are the self-hosted version of WordPress since many of them have unique functionality or a custom-made design.

Conclusion:

WordPress will provide you with all the features you need to build a powerful website. The content creation and management is really easy and you can get started in no time. With all cool features included by default and the option to extend them even more, WordPress is one of the easiest and user-friendly applications that you can use to build your website and create engaging content for your visitors.

CHAPTER 3

How to Create and Maintain a WP Site?

The first time you step foot inside the WordPress dashboard, you can't help but marvel at how simple it all appears to be. A management sidebar on the left, a clean interface to work within in the center and notifications at the top. But once you start digging deeper into WordPress, you may feel overwhelmed as you dig deeper into the layers of functionality within the content management system. So, let's talk about practical steps here.

3.1 How to Create a WP Site?

The following WordPress tutorial will walk you through all the necessary steps in setting up your first WordPress site.

- Step 1: Choose a Domain
- Step 2: Purchase Web Hosting and Domain
- Step 3: Install WordPress
- Step 4: Find a WordPress Theme
- Step 5: Install Your WordPress Theme
- Step 6: Configure Your WordPress Theme
- Step 7: Publish Your First Pages
- Step 8: Create a Menu
- Step 9: Configure Your WordPress Settings
- Step 10: Install Essential WordPress Plugins

Now, let's start the steps in detail:

3.1.1 Step 1: Choose a Domain

First and foremost, you must get a domain name for your website. Domain name is the online identity of your business, i.e. name of your website in the simple terms. In other words, it is your website address or the URL which users type on the web browser's address bar to visit your website.

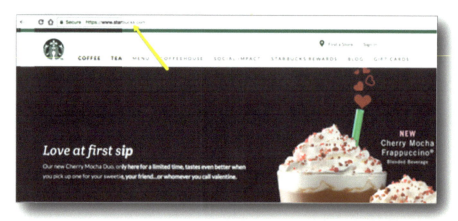

Choosing a domain name is a thoughtful task. Below are some of the things you must consider while creating/ choosing a domain name:

- **Keep it simple and short:** Create a domain name that is simple, short and easy to read, remember. It enhances the chance of users typing your website address correctly on the browser.
- **Suitable for your website content:** Make sure that your domain name is relevant to the content you are going to put on the website. Besides, you can also include keywords on the domain name if it sounds good.
- **Choose an appropriate domain extension:** Domain extension is the suffix such as .com, .net, .org, .edu, etc. which is added at the end of web addresses. They have specific meaning such as .com for commercial, .org for Organizations, and .net for network. These three extensions are the most used extensions which you can

use as per the nature of your site; however, .com is always preferred.

Besides, there are some domain name generator tools which help to create a cool brand-able domain name.

- **How to get a domain name?**

There are several domain name providers online from where you can buy a domain name. Most of the domain name providers have a domain name search tool where you can type the name you want and it checks the availability of the domain name.

Below are the top domain Registrars you can check out:

- GoDaddy
- NameCheap

3.1.2 Step 2: Purchase Web Hosting and Domain

Web hosting does exactly what it says: it "hosts" websites. In other words, web hosting companies own and manage giant web servers located in data centers around the country (and, sometimes, the world).

It's on these web servers where websites like yours sit, so you don't have to buy or manage any of the server technology yourself. You pay these companies what amounts to monthly or annual rent for space and bandwidth on the server. Then, you can focus on building your website in WordPress.

Next, you have to find out the best WordPress hosting service which suits your needs. There are several web hosting companies offering different types of WordPress hosting plans. Below are the types of WordPress hosting plans you should know about:

- **Shared Hosting:** Cheapest hosting plan. With shared hosting, multiple websites share the same IP address and resources of the server including the memory, hard disk space, and the bandwidth. (Pros: Budget-friendly plan.

Cons: Limited space, compromised speed and security)

- **VPS (Virtual Private Server):** With VPS plan, you will be provided a certain portion of server resources. You will share a server with other VPS users but there'll limited users, not as many as in shared plan. (Pros: Secure, Option to get more server resources anytime as your business grows. Cons: Expensive for the small businesses and beginners.)
- **Dedicated Hosting:** Very expensive plan. All the server resources are dedicated to a single user. (Pros: Full storage, bandwidth, and full control over the server resources, more secure. Cons: Not a cost-effective plan for small companies.)
- **Managed WordPress Hosting:** Managed WordPress hosting is hosting cum WordPress management solution which provides some of the essential WordPress tools. It is a kind of dedicated hosting specific to WordPress platform. (Pros: WordPress-centered hosting. Cons: Quite expensive for small and growing businesses.

While there isn't one clear front-runner when it comes to hosting providers, WordPress does give some solid recommendations on companies that not only work well with WordPress websites but that offer affordable hosting plans. I'd suggest you start with one of these if this is your first website.

3.1.3 Step 3: Install WordPress

There are a number of ways in which you can install WordPress. However, most web hosting providers will provide you with an easy-to-use one-click installation process that simplifies the whole process.

Using Bluehost as an example, here is what you need to do:

First, log into your new web hosting account:

You'll then arrive at your web hosting dashboard:

What you'll want to look for instead is a button that says "Install WordPress":

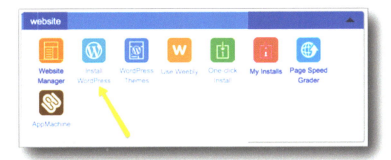

They may try to offer upgraded installation services, but there's no need for that. Simply follow the instructions for installing WordPress. Once you have completed the installation and created your WordPress login credentials, it's time to step inside. Unless you change your login domain (which you eventually should for security reasons), your admin login will be located at 'www.yourdomainname.com/wp-login.php'.

3.1.4 Step 4: Find a WordPress Theme

A WordPress theme is a pre-designed and pre-coded interface template for WordPress. Basically, it saves you the trouble (and money) of having to design your own website from-scratch or to pay someone else to do it for you.

When you log into WordPress for the first time, WordPress will automatically assign their latest theme to your site.

If you want to use a WordPress theme that works better for your niche, don't be afraid to look around and to find the best and most trustworthy WordPress theme for your purposes.

Keep in mind that every theme requires some configuration. Also, not every theme works the same way. Some utilize a basic text editor (which looks similar to the blank page in Microsoft Word) while others use a page builder or visual editor. So, switching from one theme to another will force you to do a little rework if or when you make a switch. If you want to spare yourself the possible hassle, then don't move on to the next steps until you've found the perfect WordPress theme for your site.

3.1.5 Step 5: Install Your WordPress Theme

When you find that perfect WordPress theme, it's time install it in WordPress.

- **Free WordPress Themes**

If you're using a free theme from the WordPress repository, here is what you need to do:

○ Inside WordPress, go to the Appearance tab and click on "Themes".

○ At the top of the page, click on "Add New". This will take you to the WordPress repository from within WordPress. Use this option so you don't have to do any manual installation.

○ Once you're in the repository, do a search for the WordPress theme you want to use. Hover over it, and click the "Install" button.

○ When it's done installing, you then have to activate it in order to publish it to your WordPress site.

○ Click on "Activate" (in the same spot where the "Install" button was) and wait for it to take you back into the main WordPress dashboard.

- **Premium WordPress Themes**

If you've decided to purchase a premium WordPress theme, the process will differ as third-party theme developers and marketplaces don't sync directly to WordPress. Here is what you need to do:

- ° Go to your WordPress theme's page and purchase the file. Once you've done this, you'll be taken to a screen where you can download the theme file.
- ° If there is an option for it, download the "Installable WordPress Files Only". This will give you a zipped folder you can then upload directly into WordPress.
- ° To do this, go back into WordPress, find the Appearance tab, and go to "Themes". Click on "Add New" at the top. Only, this time, you'll select the "Upload Theme" option.
- ° Select the zip file from your computer and click Install Now. With your new theme uploaded into WordPress, you can now activate and publish it to the site.

3.1.6 Step 6: Configure Your WordPress Theme

Upon activation, you'll want to spend some time configuring your theme. You can do this under the Appearance tab and then click "Customize".

Ultimately, it's up to you to decide how much or little of your theme you want to customize. However, you should at least take some time now to go through each of the modules and acquaint yourself with what you have the power to change.

- ° Site Identity is an important one to fill in, so make sure you look at that first.
- ° Colors allow to update your site to your brand's color palette (if you have one).
- ° Widgets allow you to add content to your footer.

3.1.7 Step 7: Publish Your First Pages

There are two types of "pages" you can create for your website:

- **Page**

These are traditional web pages that exist within the main navigation of a site. The About page, Contact page, and individual services pages all are made using the Page feature in WordPress.

- **Post**

These are blog post "pages" that will only exist within the blog on your website unless you designate the home page to serve as the blog feed.

Now, the great thing about WordPress is that the interface is consistent regardless of whether you're creating a page or a post. There are different settings you need to apply to each, but the main area in which you work remains the same, which makes it a workspace that's easy to get used to.

Of course, if you work in a theme that uses a page builder or a visual builder tool to create content, this is going to look a little different.

Regardless of which content creation tool your WordPress theme uses, it's time to create content for your site. If you're running a blog, simply get started writing your first Posts. Once you hit the Publish button, your blogs will go live on the designated Blog page.

3.1.8 Step 8: Create a Menu

Whereas when you hit the "Publish" button on a Post and it goes straight onto your blog, a Page needs to be added to your site's navigation (or menu) if you want it to show up.

So, the first thing to do is to create those pages for your site. Next, you'll want to go to the Appearance tab and select "Menus". This is where you will build and manage your site's navigation.

First, let's look at the menu selection dropdown. However, if your theme automatically creates secondary or footer menus for you, be sure to select the one you actually want to create/edit here. Next, let's look at the sidebar options.

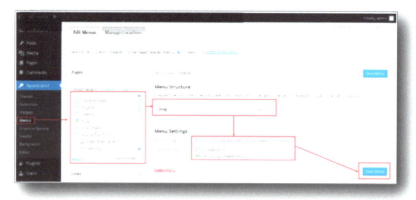

When you expand these tabs, you'll be presented with pages, posts, and other types of content that already exist on your site. Now, it's time to create your menu.

Click on the pages checkbox next to the page (or pages) you want to add to the sidebar. Then click on the "Add to Menu" button. You'll see those pages then show up under Menu Structure.

Within this interface, you can now drag-and-drop your pages and design your menu to appear however you'd like it to. You can also change the page labels that appear in the navigation. One other thing to point out here is the Menu Settings box at the bottom.

If you know that you'll be adding new pages regularly to your website and don't want to have to repeat this process every time, you can click on the "Automatically add new top-level pages to this menu" option to streamline your process. When you're done setting up your menu, save your changes.

3.1.9 Step 9: Configure Your WordPress Settings

Many of the settings offered by WordPress control things related to your pages and posts, and that's not necessarily something you'd understand until you've actually created them for your site.

So, now that you've done that, it's time to go through your settings one-by-one and make sure your WordPress site is configured to work exactly as you want it to.

- **General**
  - **Site Title:** This is what will appear in someone's browser tab when they arrive at your site.
  - **Tagline:** This can be changed when you create content for your home page, so this isn't a required field.
  - **WordPress Address:** This is the URL of your main site.
  - **Site Address:** For most of you, this will match the WordPress Address. However, if you are setting up something like Multisite that requires each site have its own sub-domain, you'll specify that here.
  - **Email Address:** This is for the main admin of your site, so they can receive all related notifications regarding it.
  - **Membership:** If you want people to subscribe to your site for updates, click this box.
  - **New User Default Role:** Keep this to Subscriber or Customer so that they can't gain access to the backend of your site.
- **Writing**
  - **Default Post Category:** If you're including a blog on your site, you should eventually come in here and remove the "Uncategorized" category. You'll want each new post to be assigned a category and removing the default setting will make it easier on yourself in the future.

- **Default Post Format:** For the most part, "Standard" should suffice unless you're using your blog to share video, audio, or image galleries.
- **Post via email:** If you want to be able to write WordPress posts and email them to your site (which I wouldn't advise), you can enable this setting here.
- **Update Services:** Leave this field be unless you have a private blog and don't want people to know when you have new content available.

- **Reading**
  - **Your homepage displays:** You have two choices when setting up a site in WordPress. You can let your homepage serve as the main blog roll so that visitors first encounter "Your latest posts". Or you can create a full-blown website and let "A static page" you created serve as the home page.
  - **A static page:** If you select this second option, you'll need to designate a page to be your homepage and a page to automatically display your posts on.
  - **Blog pages show at most:** If you show a summary of your blog posts (see option below), you can display up to 10 posts per page. If you show the full text, try to limit this to 3 posts.
  - **Syndication feeds show the most recent:** When your blog shows up in someone's RSS (syndication) feed, this setting enables you to choose how many recent posts they'll see initially.
  - **For each article in a feed, show:** This is up to you to decide, though I think a summary is probably best for improving the overall look on a main blog page's feed. It also gives visitors a reason to click through and visit another page (which is good for SEO).
  - **Search engine visibility:** Unless your website is private, do not check this box.

- **Discussion**
  - **Default article settings:** The first setting refers

to backlink notifications. The second setting refers to pingbacks and trackbacks. The third has to do with allowing comments on your blog.

- ° **Other comment settings:** If you do want visitors to leave comments, you can set requirements on who they are as well as how comments appear.
- ° **Email me whenever:** Staying engaged with people who take the time to comment on your content is a good thing. Check these so you can more easily stay on top of that.
- ° **Before a comment appears:** If you're worried about spam or abusive comments coming through, update these settings.
- ° **Comment Moderation/Blacklist:** You can decide more specifically who is allowed to leave a comment (so long as it's moderated) and who isn't.
- ° **Avatars:** If you're not running a membership site that allows users to create a full custom profile, be sure to update these settings to give your comments section a little personality.
- **Media**

If you've designed a custom WordPress site, you may have a need for custom media file sizes. In using this setting, you can streamline the media upload and sizing process. That way, visual content automatically goes into your pages at the right size and you don't have to worry about making adjustments of it in your design software or compromising visibility of the image once it's in WordPress.

3.1.10 Step 10: Install Essential WordPress Plugins

Installing WordPress plugins is the final step in the WordPress setup process.

In terms of what a WordPress plugin is, it's a piece of software that hooks into WordPress. As for what it does? Well, plugins can do a lot of different things. They can help you:

- ○ Integrate a social media feed into your site.
- ○ Resize and compress images.
- ○ Block spammers and hackers.
- ○ Create a forum.
- ○ Add a payment gateway.
- ○ Translate your site.
- ○ And much, much more.

While it's tempting to look through the WordPress repository that currently houses over 50,000 free plugins and install all of the ones that seem really cool or worthwhile, be careful. WordPress plugins are like any other kind of file or software you layer on top of your site. With more weight, comes slower loading times–and that's not something you want for your user experience.

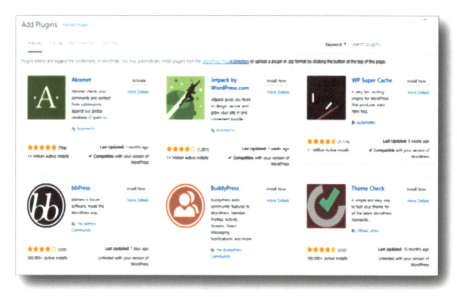

It's also important to note that some of your plugins will generate their own new tab on the sidebar. Take WP Smush, for instance. If you've chosen to use this image optimization plugin, you'll now find that it's installed a new option on your sidebar. So, be sure to look out for those new tabs after activation as they hold valuable settings and features you'll want to start accessing right away.

3.2 How to Maintain a WordPress Website?

If you want to host a successful WordPress site, you need to maintain its core functionality, installed plugins/themes, and other aspects on a regular basis. No doubt, WordPress is a great platform, but maintenance is a key that will keep you going longer across the global market.

However, maintaining a WordPress site is one of the tedious tasks, but it will help you know your efficiency, keep you updated with the latest technologies and most importantly, it remains safe and secure. So make sure you follow the right maintenance tactics that will boost the security, performance, and functionality of your site to a great extent. So, let's take a look:

1. **Backup your site regularly:** This is the most vital things that you need to do on a regular basis. Although backing up don't keep your site fresh and clean, it helps if something goes wrong as you can revert to a previous version immediately. Backup your WordPress site on a monthly basis. You can also backup your blogs daily, while, weekly backups are good for corporate sites. You can back-up your site via your hosting provider or by downloading a local copy of your site through FTP.

2. **Keep your site up-to-date:** If you want to maintain your site, you should update your core WordPress, installed themes and plugins to its latest version on a frequent basis. Fortunately, WordPress rolls out its latest version 4.6 frequently to offer their users more advanced features and security fixes.

All you need is to log in to your WordPress site on a monthly basis and update the core WP, themes, and plugins.

3. **Delete Unused plugins:** WordPress plugins are a great way to extend the functionality of the site. But using too many plugins could affect the performance as well as the security of a website.

If you want a successful site, you need to remove all those

plugins that you haven't used till now. In short, get rid of the plugins that you don't need. For that, you first need to deactivate the plugin, and then delete it. But before this, take a look at every plugin you have installed to find out the unused plugins.

4. **Optimize your database:** A database is a place where all your site content is stored. It includes your blog posts, pages, images, videos, setting and much more. As your site grows, your database begins to get bloated, which in turn slow down the speed of your site.

If you want to improve the performance of your site, you need to optimize your database. With the help of WordPress plugin (such as WP-Optimize that will automatically optimize your database and clears records that are now not required), you can optimize the database of your site and enhance its speed.

5. **Focus on your site's security:** Most of the WordPress users overlook the security of their site. But it is one of the crucial factors that need to be considered. If you want to secure your site from hackers and other security threats, you need to install a reliable security plugin. You can use the iThemes Security plugin that will protect your site from hackers within a few clicks. In fact, you should also use a Sucuri service to monitor your site.

6. **Keep an eye on your site's speed:** If you want to attract more visitors, you need to provide them fast loading pages. This means the speed of a site directly affect the ranking of your site on search engines. In fact, Google prefers fast loading sites. So, you should know the loading speed of your site.

Luckily, there is Google's Page Speed Insights that offers a tool to grade your site's load time, and then offers tips to improve it. You can install this tool and improve the performance of your site within a few clicks.

7. **Manage user accounts:** The security of your site is also based on the aspect that how you manage your user

accounts. Most of the website owners doll out their site's password and leave it vulnerable. If you are a newbie user, you should avoid giving your login details to your multiple users. Each user should have their own login and password details as it gives more security to the site. Apart from this, make sure you don't use "admin" username for your WP account. Try to swap the default username with the new and unique one. You can also use the lengthy and difficult-to-break password. Plus, you can also change the URL of your login page if you want to protect your site from hackers and other security threats.

Conclusion:

WordPress is the undisputed champ of content management systems, which is why there's never been a better time to learn how to use it. In just 10 steps (and some careful research and planning), you can get your first WordPress website up and running! Good luck!

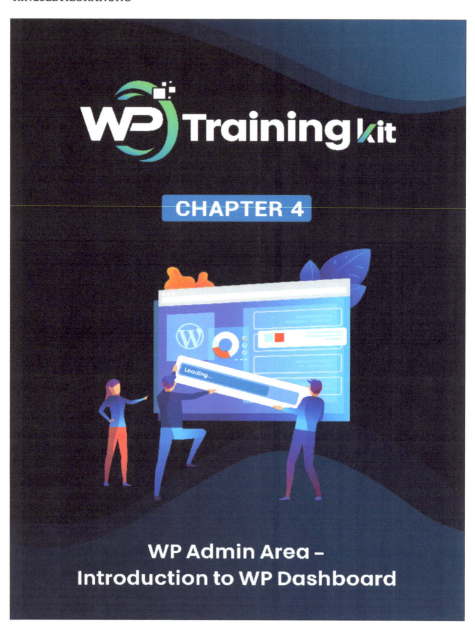

CHAPTER 4

WP Admin Area –
Introduction to WP Dashboard

Once you've logged into your WordPress site via the login form, you should be presented with the WordPress Dashboard, which is your site's admin area. WordPress dashboard is the interface where administrators or other users manage website page, posts and perform other tasks. So let's dig right in…

4.1 What is the WordPress Dashboard?

WordPress dashboard is the interface that appears when you log in to your WordPress website by appending wp-admin to the URL of your website. Hence if your website is https://www.example.com/ The WordPress dashboard login URL for this website would be https://www.example.com/wp-admin/

The dashboard contains various settings which help you set up your website efficiently and modify several aspects of your site without needing to FTP to your site or touch the WordPress database.

Your WordPress administration section is where all of your site's administration is controlled from. Your Dashboard is divided into several areas that provide you with access to tools and features such as:

- Useful data and information about what is taking place on your site. It also provides you with "at-a-glance" metrics and reports about recent activity taking place on your site, system updates, and notifications, and to be kept updated on the latest news from the WordPress community and various WordPress-related resources, such as notifications and announcements from WordPress product vendors of plugins and themes that you have installed on your site.
- Management and control of all website settings and options.
- Features that let you modify, expand, update and

enhance the design and functionality of your site, upgrade plugins and themes, and add, modify and delete content or content sections.

In version 3.8, WordPress introduced new design changes to its backend section …

Even though this new design was mostly cosmetic and aimed at giving WordPress users and developers cleaner typography for a better optimized mobile and desktop viewing experience and a more aesthetic experience, it also affected much of the existing WordPress documentation around the web, including thousands of tutorials and articles about WordPress online, in print and on video that are now in need of being updated.

4.2 Your WordPress Dashboard

Depending on whether you or someone else manages your site, you may or may not see the messages below. The first time you log into your WordPress site, you may see a "Welcome to WordPress" message displayed at the top of the Dashboard…

If you are new to using your website and want to spend a little time learning more about WordPress, just click on the "Get Started" or "Next Step" links. To dismiss the "Welcome" message or prevent it from showing again inside your admin area the next time you log in, click on the Dismiss link near the top right-hand corner of the page…

Feel free to explore the information displayed in the "welcome" message if you want to learn about new features and updates to the software. To go back to the dashboard, just select "Dashboard" (or click on Dashboard > Home) on the admin menu section…

Or scroll down to the bottom of the page and click on the link to dismiss the message and return to your main Dashboard…

4.3 WordPress Dashboard Screen Areas

Your Dashboard gives you access to all of the main controls and features that you will need to administrate the site…

Your main Dashboard screen is divided into the following sections:

- Header And Toolbar Section (1)
- Main Navigation Menu (2)
- Work Area (3)
- Footer Section (4)

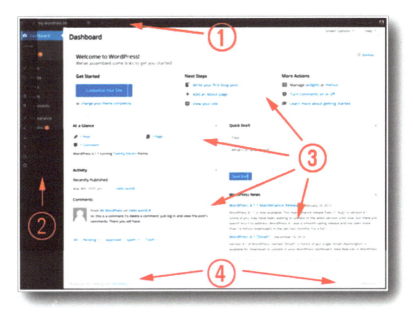

4.3.1 WordPress Dashboard Area: Header Section

The header section displays system updates, messages, warnings and notifications. A whole range of updates, messages, banner, announcements, notifications, and warnings can display on your header, depending on what area you are working on, what action has been performed, or which plugins you have installed on your site.

- ### Screen Options Feature

The Screen Options tab is located in the top-right corner of your WordPress administration screen, in the header section. Clicking on this tab displays different options and features on your screen, depending on which section of the administration backend you are currently working on.

For example, if you are in the main Dashboard, clicking on the Screen Options tab allows you to configure options like which panels of your Dashboard screen you want to hide or display. If you are in the Posts section of your site management area, clicking on the Screen Options tab lets you select totally different options, such as displaying or hiding information in the listings section (e.g. tags, comments, etc.), specifying the number of posts to display per page, and other configurable options depending on the plugins you have installed on your site.

- **Online Help Section**

You can access the official WordPress documentation and user help forum sections by clicking on the Help tab located on the top right-hand corner of your header area.

Like the Screen Options tab, the Help tab also displays context-specific information. So, for example, if you are editing content in the Edit Post area, clicking on the Help tab will bring up help information and tutorials relevant to editing posts.

4.3.2 WP Admin Area: Toolbar

The Toolbar displays at the very top of your Dashboard screen and provides you and your logged in site users with access to a range of important administration functions, features, information and "quick links" to other areas of your site. Most Toolbar items can expand to display additional information by hovering your mouse over the icons.

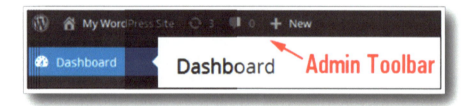

For example, the "updates" icon on the toolbar lets you see if the WordPress software or any plugins or themes need to be updated. You can also see at a glance how many comments are awaiting moderation, create new posts or pages, add new media or links into your content, add new users to your site and a whole lot more.

4.3.3 WordPress Admin Area: Navigation Menu

On the left side of the Dashboard is the main navigation menu that contains links to all the administrative functions that you can perform on your website.

Keep in mind that what users see inside the Dashboard area when logged in depends on the role and capabilities assigned to them and how the site administrator has configured settings and options for different features.

In order to access all of the WP control area features, you must be an administrator of the site.

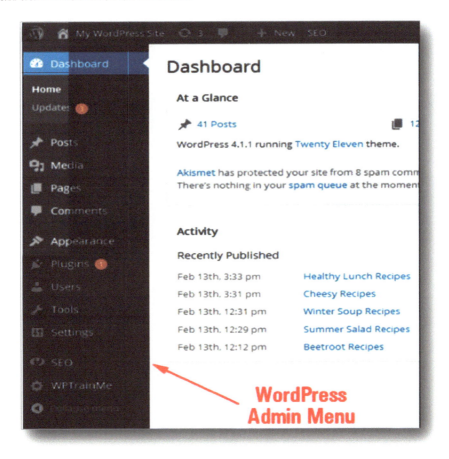

Users with roles other than that of an administrator (e.g. "Subscriber", "Author", etc.) get access to fewer menu options inside the dashboard.

Irrespective of the role assigned to a user, some admin menu items like "Collapse menu" remain accessible to all. Click the Collapse menu button at the bottom of the menu bar.

And the admin menu collapses into a narrow band with only a set of icons displaying for all functions.

This is a useful feature if you want more space in your admin working area. If you are working with the collapsed menu and are not sure what the icons mean, just click the bottom icon to expand all items, or hover over an icon to display its submenus.

If you hover your mouse over a menu item, a submenu will fly out. To stick" sub-menus into the navigation menu bar while you're working, click on a menu item.

4.3.4 WordPress Admin Area: Working Area

The large area in the middle of your admin screen is your main work area. This is where you will get access to most of your site's information, do most of your admin work, create, modify and delete pages, posts and content related to these, upload images and media to your site, add, update and configure plugins and themes, change your site options, etc.

When you log into your site, your Dashboard displays a number of panels with information about various activities taking place on your site, including updates and notices from several sources.

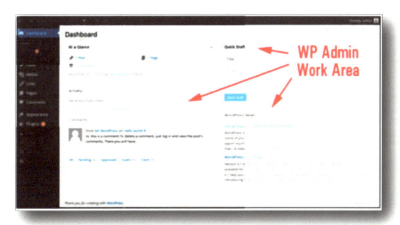

As you get busier and start adding more content and functionality (e.g. adding e-commerce or a support helpdesk, etc.) and more users begin to interact with your site, this section will start looking very busy.

Fortunately, you can customize your admin area by hiding, minimizing and reorganizing the layout and display of your information sections. For a quick and easy tutorial on ways to customize your WordPress Dashboard, go here: Customizing The WordPress Dashboard Section.

4.3.5 WordPress Administration Area: Footer

The footer section is found at the bottom of your WP Dashboard area and displays a link to WordPress and your site's current WordPress software version.

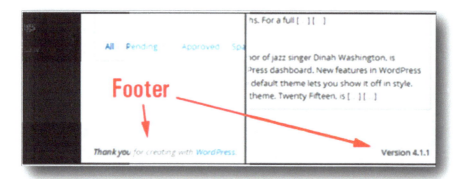

Conclusion:

As you can see there is a lot of useful information on the WordPress Dashboard that you can use. So make full use of the Dashboard.

WordPress Plugins allows you to easily modify, customize, and enhance a WordPress site. Instead of changing the core program code of WordPress, you can add functionality with WordPress Plugins.

If you're new to WordPress, you might find yourself wondering, "what is a WordPress plugin?". It's a fairly common question to ask because, in addition to being one of the many new terms that WordPress will introduce to your vocabulary, plugins are also an essential building block of every single WordPress site. Here is a basic definition.

5.1 WordPress Plug-ins

A plugin is a piece of software containing a group of functions that can be added to a WordPress website. They can extend functionality or add new features to your WordPress websites.

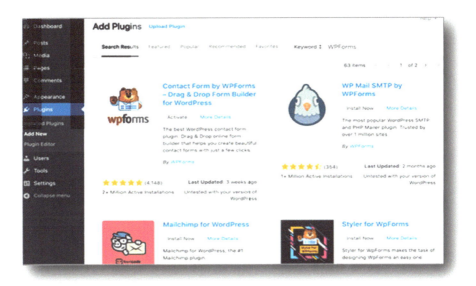

WordPress plugins are written in the PHP programming language and integrate seamlessly with WordPress. In the WordPress community, there is a saying that goes around: "there's a plugin for that". They make it easier for users to add features to their website without knowing a single line of code.

There are thousands of WordPress plugins available for free at the official WordPress plugin directory. Aside from free plugins, there are tons of amazing commercial ones available from third-party companies and developers.

As a site administrator, you can install/uninstall plugins from the admin area. You can also download and manually install them using an FTP client.

Because the vast majority of plugins are free, it is important to note that they usually do not come with tech support. For this reason, it is important to be careful when choosing which ones you want to install on your site.

Although there are plugins that can do the task you want them to do, some are much higher quality than others. In order to choose the right ones, you should ask yourself a couple of questions.

How long has it been since it was updated? Is it compatible with the latest version of WordPress? Are people getting answers to their support questions? What type of rating does it have?

There is a myth that WordPress plugins slow your site down. It is not true. Only the number of bad ones will slow down your site.

5.2 How to Install a WordPress Plugin – Step by Step for Beginners

After installing WordPress, the first thing every beginner needs to learn is how to install a WordPress plugin. Plugins allow you to add new features to WordPress such as add a gallery, slideshow, etc. There are thousands of free and paid plugins available for WordPress. But before you start, if you are using WordPress.com, then you cannot install plugins. WordPress.com has its limitations. You cannot install plugins on WordPress.com unless you upgrade to their business plan. On the other hand, you can install any plugin you want on your self-hosted WordPress.org website right out of the box.

Installing a WordPress plugin involves three methods:

- Installing a WordPress plugin using search
- Uploading a WordPress plugin
- Manually installing a WordPress plugin using FTP

5.2.1 Install a Plugin using WordPress Plugin Search

The easiest way of installing a WordPress plugin is to use the plugin search. The only downside of this option is that a plugin must be in the WordPress plugin directory which is limited to only free plugins.

First thing you need to do is go to your WordPress admin area and click on Plugins » Add New.

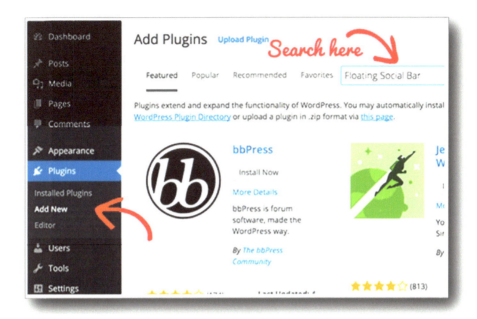

You will see a screen like the one in the screenshot above. Find the plugin by typing the plugin name or the functionality you are looking for like we did. After that, you will see a bunch of listings like the example below:

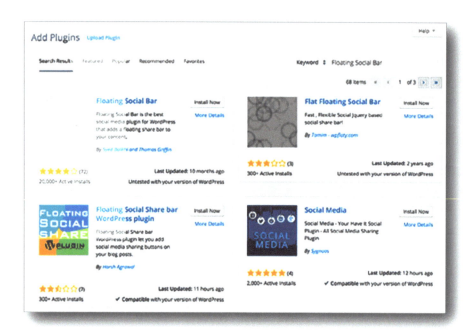

You can pick the plugin that is best for you. Since in our search, we were looking for Floating Social Bar which happens to be the first plugin, we will click the 'Install Now' button. WordPress will now download and install the plugin for you. After this, you will see the success message with a link to activate the plugin or return to plugin installer.

A WordPress plugin can be installed on your site, but it will not work unless you activate it. So go ahead and click on the activate plugin link to activate the plugin on your WordPress site. That's all; you have successfully installed your first WordPress plugin.

The next step is to configure the plugin settings. These settings will vary for each plugin, therefore, it cannot be discussed in general.

5.2.2 Install a Plugin using the WordPress Admin Plugin Upload

Paid WordPress plugins are not listed in the WordPress plugin directory. These plugins cannot be installed using the first method.

That's why WordPress has the Upload method to install such plugins. We will explore how to install WordPress plugins using the upload option in the admin area.

First, you need to download the plugin from the source (which will be a zip file). Next, you need to go to the WordPress admin area and visit Plugins » Add New page.

After that, click on the Upload Plugin button on top of the page.

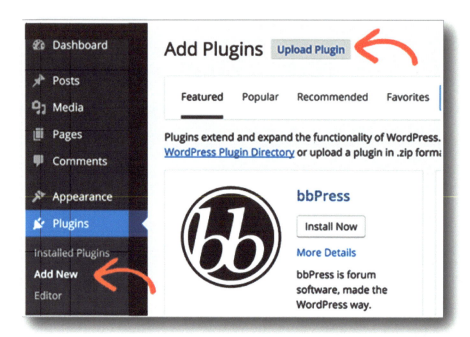

This will bring you to the plugin upload page. Here you need to click on the choose file button and select the plugin file you downloaded earlier to your computer.

After you have selected the file, you need to click on the install now button.

WordPress will now upload the plugin file from your computer and install it for you. You will see a success message like this after the installation is finished.

Installing Plugin from uploaded file: envira-gallery.zip

Unpacking the package...

Installing the plugin...

Plugin installed successfully.

Activate Plugin | Return to Plugins page

Once installed, you need to click on the Activate Plugin link to start using the plugin.

You would have to configure the settings to fit your needs. These settings will vary for each plugin, therefore, it cannot be discussed in general terms.

5.2.3 Manually Install a WordPress Plugin using FTP

In some cases, your WordPress hosting provider may have file restrictions that could limit your ability to install a plugin from the admin area.

In this situation, your best bet is to install the plugin manually using FTP. The FTP manager method is the least friendly for beginners.

First, you will need to download the plugin's source file (it will be a zip file). Next, you need to extract the zip file on your computer.

Extracting the plugin zip file will create a new folder with the same name. This is the folder that you need to manually upload to your website using an FTP client.

You would need to access your host through the FTP manager. If you do not have your FTP username and password, then contact your WordPress hosting provider and ask them.

Open the FTP client on your computer and connect to your website using the login credentials provided by your web host. Once connected, you need to access the path /wp-content/ plugins/

Next, upload the folder you extracted from the zip file to the /wp-content/plugins/ folder on your web server.

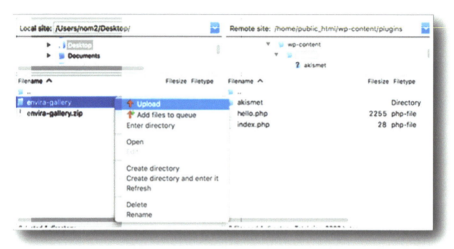

After uploading the files, you need to visit the WordPress admin area and click on the Plugins link in the admin menu. You will see your plugin successfully installed on the plugins page.

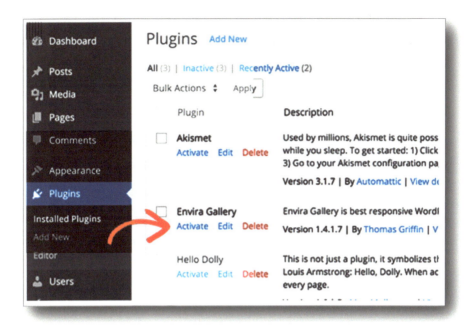

You need to click on the Activate link below the plugin. Upon activating, you may need to configure the plugin settings. WordPress plugins come with their own settings which differ from one plugin to another.

5.3 Best WordPress Plugins for Your Site

Having the right set of WordPress plugins and tools can help you grow your online business. There are all-star plugins that can help with content strategy, SEO, site security and even Facebook Messenger marketing.

There are over 54,000+ WordPress plugins that you can choose from. This makes it extremely overwhelming for new users to find the right plugin for their website.

Here we have the list of 10 best WordPress plugins to add to your website:

1. MobileMonkey's WP-Chatbot

Want to connect your business with the 1.3 billion+ users on Facebook Messenger?

Then power your site with MobileMonkey's WP-Chatbot.
It's just like a traditional website chat where users can chat
with a support team or get answers to questions, but with the
added benefit of getting information on every single one of
those users.

When a user chats with a MobileMonkey-powered site chat,
the conversation they're having is being facilitated through
Facebook Messenger.
That's means every chat bubble conversation will have a
history.
More importantly, you can add forms where users can
automatically add their information, making it simple for
you to gather data on your customers and follow up with
them.

2. Yoast SEO

This is one of the best on-page SEO plugins for WordPress
sites. Yoast SEO shows how SEO-friendly your post is and
gives recommendations for how to improve it. Among other
things, it will analyze your keyword use, your metadata, and
the readability of your content.

3. Jetpack

It's the all-in-one features package for every WordPress site, made by the WordPress team. Jetpack is a must-have plugin, giving WordPress users numerous powerful features.

It takes care of website security, performance, traffic growth, image optimization, design, etc.

4. Akismet Anti-Spam

This plugin tends to be automatically installed along with WordPress. Akismet is your main safeguard against spam comments on your WordPress site.

It filters out comments that are spammy with illicit links, inappropriate messages, and such. You can also see a status history for each comment, so you can know where they come from. If you need more powerful features for a commercial website, there's a premium option.

5. WooCommerce

If you're looking to build an online store, then this is the

WordPress plugin you should install. WooCommerce is the No. 1 plugin for e-commerce in WordPress.

You can install it and easily set it up to add product listings and shopping cart in your website. It has features for providing customers with multiple options in shipping, payment methods, etc. There is also an online community of WooCommerce users worldwide you can interact with.

6. Wordfence Security

Website security is something most people take for granted -; until they get hacked. This WordPress plugin guard against hacking with real-time monitoring and protection.

It also has firewall protection, malware scan, blocking, login security, and many other features. Wordfence also logs real-time activities on your website, so you can always keep an eye on things.

7. Google XML Sitemaps

Setting up Google XML sitemaps and getting them just right can be tedious. This plugin creates your XML sitemap for you and ensures your website will be indexed by all the major search engines.

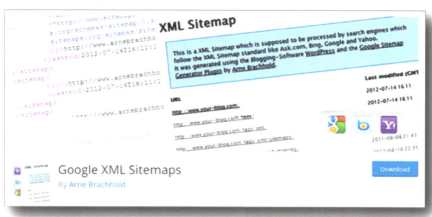

Save time and effort in your website's SEO initial setup with this plugin.

8. WPForms

If you need to add forms in posts and pages, nothing comes

close to WPForms. It's the most beginner-friendly plugin for building forms in WordPress. WPForms has a drag-and-drop interface that lets you create a contact form easily.

This plugin has a lite version you can try out and keep using for free if it satisfies your needs. If you want more features, then you can go for the pro version. That paid version lets you collect payments, conduct surveys, take job applications, and so on.

9. MonsterInsights

This plugin makes your Google Analytics visible through your WordPress dashboard. It's quick and easy to connect Google Analytics, and once it's set up, it's so convenient to see your data within Wordpress.

There's a 100% free lite version (woot!), as well as a pro version with more robust metrics for publisher and e-commerce sites.

10.   Redirection

There may be times you have to change the permalinks of your posts or pages. But every now and then, you forget to redirect them since that can get pretty tedious.

This aptly-named plugin lets you manage all the 301 redirects and 404 errors in your site. You can then redirect all those faulty URLs and have full logs of all the redirects. This plugin is especially useful when you make big changes to your WordPress site.

Conclusion:

Plugins are the add-ons that enable you to expand your site's functionality and make it do just about anything you'd like. You can find plugins that help you build and optimize your site, maintain it over time, and add new features such as contact forms and storefronts.

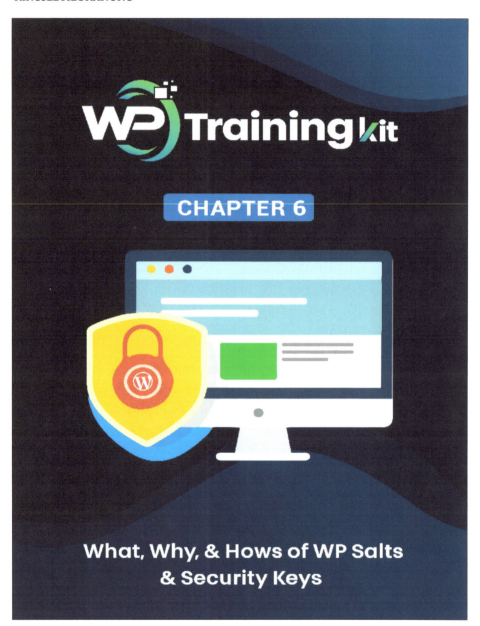

When it comes to protecting your WordPress website, the login screen is an important line of defense. A significant part of this is making sure your password is secure, which makes it far less likely that attackers will be able to crack it and gain access.

Despite the measures you take to implement good login practices, leaving your site's security to users is not a good idea. This is why WordPress uses a set of security keys or secret keys. Let's find out about them…

6.1 What Are WordPress Security Keys & Salts?

WordPress Security Keys is a set of random variables that improve encryption of information stored in the user's cookies. There are a total of four security keys:

- AUTH_KEY
- SECURE_AUTH_KEY
- LOGGED_IN_KEY
- NONCE_KEY

Salt keys are cryptographic elements used to 'hash' data in order to secure it. In fact, most serious platforms and systems use similar mechanisms to protect sensitive data. The process works by using the salt keys to encrypt your password when you save it in WordPress. This way, attackers can't see your passwords in plaintext even if they somehow gain access to your database.

Salt keys are also used to sign your website's cookies. This stops malicious actors from being able to gain access even if they can take over your cookies. All of this happens in the background, and there are zero reasons why you'd ever need to share your WordPress salt keys with a third party. If someone were to get their hands on them, they'd might be able to use them in order to access your passwords and crack your website.

You can find both WP salts and security keys in the wpconfig.php file. WordPress generates four security keys and salts in the wp-config.php file. After a fresh WordPress install, this is how the WordPress secret keys and salts look:

- define('AUTH_KEY', 'put your unique phrase here');
- define('SECURE_AUTH_KEY', 'put your unique phrase here');
- define('LOGGED_IN_KEY', 'put your unique phrase here');
- define('NONCE_KEY', 'put your unique phrase here');
- define('AUTH_SALT', 'put your unique phrase here');
- define('SECURE_AUTH_SALT', 'put your unique phrase

here');
- define('LOGGED_IN_SALT', 'put your unique phrase here');
- define('NONCE_SALT', 'put your unique phrase here');

You need to generate security keys and WordPress salts and replace the 'put your unique phrase here' with random variables you just generated.

6.2 How Does WordPress Salts and Security Keys Work?

Unlike most of other websites platforms, WordPress does not use the PHP sessions to keep track of their users. To verify an identity of logged in users as well as commenters, WordPress usually uses the cookies or information that are stored in your browser's history. When you log in to your Dashboard multiple cookies are created and saved. Usually, the two cookies that are created are:

- WordPress_[hash]
- wordpress_logged_in_[hash]

The first one is used only when you are logged onto your Dashboard while the second cookie is used throughout WordPress to ensure whether or not you are logged in. The details you use to log in are hashed (assigned cryptic values) using the random variables which are then specified in the WordPress security keys. This, in turn, strengthens and makes it almost impossible for anyone to guess your password should your cookies be stolen.

6.3 How to Use WordPress Security Keys and Salts?

Usually, when your WordPress websites are self-hosted, the security keys are not pre-defined. Instead, you might need to generate and add them yourself. But don't worry, the process is quite simple and straightforward. Generally, there are two ways you can configure the secret key. We will be discussing both methods for your convenience so you can choose whichever method you prefer.

- Manually change the WordPress Security Keys and Salts

- Using a WordPress Plugin

Method 1: Manually Changing the Secret Keys & Salts!

Follow the steps below as a guideline and secure your WordPress profile and website!

You can easily change WordPress security keys and salts. The WordPress Foundation provides a WordPress key generator that creates random values for secret keys and salts. Visit the following link: https://api.wordpress.org/secret-key/1.1/salt/

Copy the values you get from the link and then paste it in your wp-config file.

Step 1: To access the wp-config.php, open your web host account and go cPanel. Select File Manager, and it'll take you to a page that looks somewhat like this:

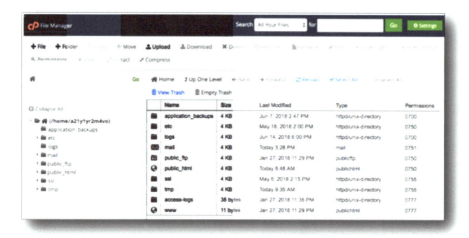

Step 2: On the left-hand side, you can see the public_html folder where you'll find the wp-config file.

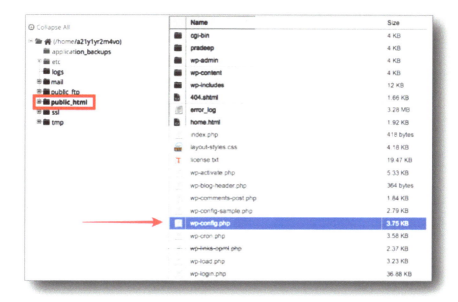

STEP 3: RIGHT CLICK ON THE FILE AND SELECT EDIT.

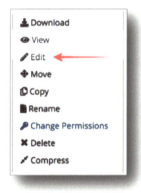

Replace the 'put your unique phrase here' with the variables you just generated.

And that's it. That's how you generate and insert unique keys and WordPress salts on your website.

Method 2: Using a Plugin

For explaining this method more thoroughly we will be using the help of the plugin- Salt Shaker. A Free WordPress security plugin, Salt Shaker is also extremely user-friendly! So to start off the process Install and Activate the plugin.

Once the plugin is activated and ready to use, you will find a newly added menu on the Tools section as Salt Shaker.

After you click on the menu, you will be redirected to a new page that features the option to set a schedule for changing the SALT keys. Go ahead and tick off the option to Change WP Keys and Salts.

You will also see the option to either choose a Daily, Weekly or Monthly basis to schedule the change of keys and salts. Select the option you prefer and your settings are saved.

In case you want to change the WordPress security keys and salts immediately, you can also see an option for Change Now on the bottom of the page. Note that once you change the keys you will be automatically logged out of your WordPress.

Conclusion:

Storing passwords in plaintext is always a bad idea, and that's where salt keys come in. WordPress uses unique salt keys to secure your passwords, which stop attackers from accessing your passwords even if they were to gain access to your database. You can ensure that these are even more secure by changing them regularly.

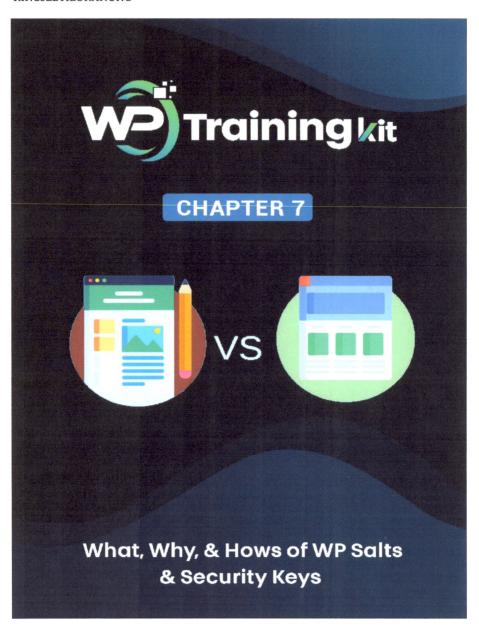

Often WordPress beginners get confused between posts and pages. By default, WordPress comes with two content types: posts and pages.

As a beginner, you are probably wondering what's the difference between posts vs pages. They seem to look similar in the WordPress dashboard as well as on the website.

7.1 What are Posts in WordPress?

Posts are blog content listed in reverse chronological order (newest content on top). You will see posts listed on your blog page. If you are using WordPress as a blog, then you will end up using posts for the majority of your website's content.

You can add and edit your WordPress posts from the 'Posts' menu in your dashboard. Here is how Add New Post screen looks.

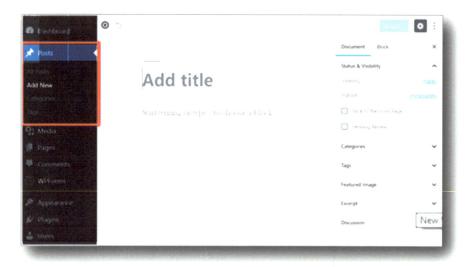

Due to their reverse chronological order, your posts are meant to be timely. Older posts are archived based on month and year. As the posts get older, the user has to dig deeper to find them. You have the option to organize your posts based on categories and tags.

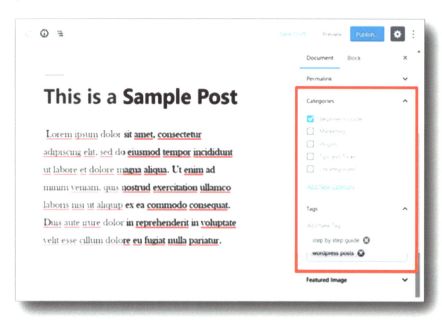

Because WordPress posts are published with time and date in mind, they are syndicated through the RSS feeds. This allows your readers to be notified of the most recent post update via RSS feeds.

Bloggers can use the RSS feeds to deliver email broadcasts through services like Constant Contact, Aweber or MailChimp. You can create a daily and weekly newsletter for your audience to subscribe to.

The very timely nature of posts makes it extremely social. You can use one of the many social sharing plugins to allow your users to share your posts on social media networks like Facebook, Twitter, LinkedIn, Pinterest, etc.

Posts encourage conversation. They have a built-in comment feature that allows users to comment on a particular topic. By default, comments, pingbacks, and trackbacks are enabled.

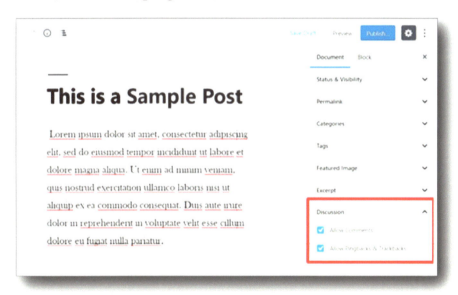

You can go to your Settings » Discussion to turn off comments on older posts if you like. WordPress posts usually have the name of the author and published/updated date.

After the main article content, there is the comments section. You cannot usually find these on a page. Now that you know what are posts, let's take a look at pages and how they are different.

7.2 What are Pages in WordPress?

Pages are static "one-off" type content such as your about page, privacy policy, contact page, etc. While the WordPress database stores the published date of the page, pages are timeless entities.

For example, your about page is not supposed to expire. Sure you can go back and make updates to it, but chances are you will not have about page 2012, about page 2013, etc. Because there is no time and date tied to pages, they are not included in your RSS feeds by default.

You can add and edit pages in WordPress from the 'Pages' menu in your dashboard. Here is how Add New Page screen looks like:

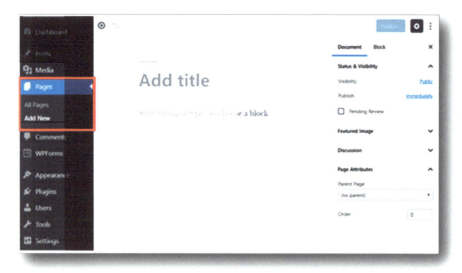

Pages are not meant to be social in most cases thus do not include social sharing buttons. For example, you probably don't want others to tweet your privacy policy page in most cases.

Similarly, pages also don't include comments. You don't want users to comment on your contact page or your legal disclaimers page. There is an option to enable comments, however, it is disabled by default for your WordPress pages.

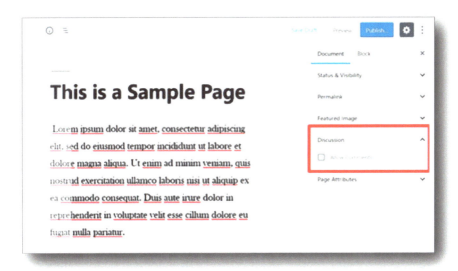

Unlike posts, pages are hierarchical by nature. For example, you can have subpages or child pages within a page. You can easily turn a page into subpage by choosing a parent page from Page Attributes when editing a page.

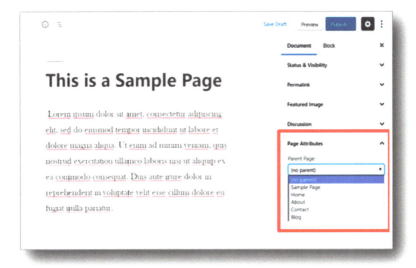

A key example of this in action would be our Blueprint page. This feature allows you to organize your pages together, and even assign a custom template to them.

WordPress by default comes with a feature that allows you to create custom page templates using your theme. This allows developers to customize the look of each page when necessary.

In most themes, post and pages look the same. But when you are using your page to create a landing page or a gallery page, then the custom page templates feature comes in very handy.

Pages also have this archaic feature called 'Order' which lets you customize the order of pages by assigning a number value to it. However, this feature is extended by plugins like Simple Page Ordering that allows you to drag & drop the order of pages.

7.3 When to Use WordPress Pages

If your content ticks both of these boxes, its recommend using a WordPress Page:

- the content will not be updated frequently
- the content will remain relevant for a long period of time

Here are a few examples of when you should use WordPress Pages (instead of Posts):

If your company offers a handful of products or services, it should be created using Pages:

- About, services, contact, legal and privacy pages are best formatted as WordPress Pages
- Use Pages when you want to group content so it fits in a parent–>child, (hierarchical) relationship, or if you want to customize the URL structure
  - yoursite.com/services/marketing/
  - yoursite.com/services/web-design/

7.4 When to Use WordPress Posts

If you are not going to post regular news or updates about your business, chances are you won't use Posts at all. A simple business website, with a homepage, about, services & contact page, does not need to use WordPress Posts.

Here are a few examples of when you should use WordPress Posts (instead of Pages):

- Your personal blog should use Posts to publish regular articles about travel, adventures, your fitness journey, rock collection, funny things your dog does, etc. Any specific topic that you plan to write about regularly should be a Post.
- Company events, announcements, conferences attended, etc. on your business website should be Posts. These are date-sensitive pieces of content.
- Press releases should almost always be Posts, not Pages.
- All content that you want to be syndicated via WordPress' built-in RSS feed should use a Post
- All other pieces of content that will be published regularly and centered around a common theme or topic

As a general rule of thumb, if you're not blogging or adding new content to your site on a regular basis, just use pages.

Sometimes WordPress includes one sample Post and a sample comment. If you're only using Pages, you should delete both the Post and the comment so they don't show up in search engines.

7.5 Features of Both WordPress Pages & Posts

Both Pages & Posts have several things in common:

- There's no limit to the number of Pages or Posts you create
- They both include a page title
- They both provide all standard content editing tools that WordPress offers (text, lists, headings, alignment, etc.)
- You can add images and/or embed video
- Both Pages & Posts allow you to set a featured image
- They both support custom fields
- They both support comments & trackbacks, although typically these are only shown on Posts
- They both allow you to choose the author of the content, although they're typically only shown on Posts
- They both maintain a publish date, although this is typically only shown on Posts
- You can set their visibility to the public, password-protected or private
- Revisions are kept for both WordPress Pages & Posts
- Custom layout templates can be used for both
- You can preview your content before making it live
- You can schedule content to publish at a later time

7.6 WordPress Pages vs. Posts (Key Differences)

To summarize, the following are the key differences between posts vs pages in WordPress.

- Posts are timely vs. Pages are timeless.
- Posts are social vs. Pages are NOT.
- Posts are organized using categories and tags vs. Pages are hierarchical and can be organized as child and parent pages.
- Posts are included in RSS feed vs. Pages are not.
- Posts have author and published date vs Pages do not.

The differences we listed above may have exceptions. You can use plugins to extend the functionality of both content types.

Conclusion:

Despite these differences, there are some similarities between pages and posts in WordPress. First, they are both used for publishing content. You can add text, images, forms, etc. to both posts and pages. There is featured image meta-field in both pages and posts.

You can build a website without ever using posts or blogging features of WordPress. You can also make a business website with pages and a separate blog section for your news, announcements, and other articles.

CHAPTER 8

Deploying security measures
in WordPress

WordPress security is a topic of huge importance for every website owner. Google blacklists around 10,000+ websites every day for malware and around 50,000 for phishing every week. If you are serious about your website, then you need to pay attention to the WordPress security best practices.

While WordPress core software is very secure, and it's audited regularly by hundreds of developers, there is a lot that can be done to keep your site secure. The security is not just about risk elimination. It's also about risk reduction. As a website owner, there's a lot that you can do to improve your WordPress security (even if you're not tech-savvy).

We have a number of actionable steps that you can take to protect your website against security vulnerabilities.

8.1 Basics of WordPress Security

8.1.1 Why WordPress security is so important?

At its core WordPress is very secure; the CMS is audited by hundreds of expert coders who write security into WordPress. Nonetheless, WordPress can still be hacked and often it is due to a lack of basic security practices.

WordPress sites that are hacked can be very damaging for the owner as it inevitably leads to a loss of reputation while also leading to financial loss. A hacker can rob a business of its confidential user data, can install software that leads to further damage down the road or even install malicious programs on your user's PCs.

Google plays a strong role in policing websites. First, it can exclude potentially hacked websites from search results – and indeed it blacklists tens of thousands of sites every week. Google also warns users away from infected sites by displaying a warning in Chrome. The resulting warnings can lead to a huge drop in traffic for website owners.

The responsibility for securing a website lies, of course, with the website owner. It's no different from business security at a physical place of business. Essentially, your website is your premises and you need to ensure that it is secured.

8.1.2 Keeping WordPress Updated

WordPress is open-source software which is regularly maintained and updated. By default, WordPress automatically installs minor updates. For major releases, you need to manually initiate the update.

WordPress also comes with thousands of plugins and themes that you can install on your website. These plugins and themes are maintained by third-party developers which regularly release updates as well.

These WordPress updates are crucial for the security and stability of your WordPress site. You need to make sure that your WordPress core, plugins, and theme are up to date.

8.1.3 Strong Passwords and User Permissions

The most common WordPress hacking attempts to use stolen passwords. You can make that difficult by using stronger passwords that are unique for your website. Not just for the WordPress admin area, but also for FTP accounts, database, WordPress hosting account, and your custom email addresses which use your site's domain name.

Many beginners don't like using strong passwords because they're hard to remember. The good thing is that you don't need to remember passwords anymore. You can use a password manager.

Another way to reduce the risk is to not give anyone access to your WordPress admin account unless you absolutely have to. If you have a large team or guest authors, then make sure that you understand user roles and capabilities in WordPress before you add new user accounts and authors to your WordPress site.

8.1.4 The Role of WordPress Hosting

Your WordPress hosting service plays the most important role in the security of your WordPress site. A good shared hosting provider like Bluehost or Site ground takes the extra measures to protect their servers against common threats.

Here is how a good web hosting company works in the background to protect your websites and data.

- They continuously monitor their network for suspicious activity
- All good hosting companies have tools in place to prevent large scale DDOS attacks
- They keep their server software and hardware up to date

to prevent hackers from exploiting a known security vulnerability in an old version
- They have ready to deploy disaster recovery and accidents plans which allows them to protect your data in case of a major accident

On a shared hosting plan, you share the server resources with many other customers. This opens the risk of cross-site contamination where a hacker can use a neighboring site to attack your website.

Using a managed WordPress hosting service provides a more secure platform for your website. Managed WordPress hosting companies offer automatic backups, automatic WordPress updates, and more advanced security configurations to protect your website.

8.2 WordPress Security in Easy Steps (No Coding)

We know that improving WordPress security can be a terrifying thought for beginners. Especially if you're not techy. We will learn how you can improve your WordPress security with just a few clicks (no coding required).

If you can point-and-click, you can do this!

8.2.1 Install a WordPress Backup Solution

Backups are your first defense against any WordPress attack. Remember, nothing is 100% secure. If government websites can be hacked, then so can yours.

Backups allow you to quickly restore your WordPress site in case something bad was to happen.

There are many free and paid WordPress backup plugins that you can use. The most important thing you need to know when it comes to backups is that you must regularly save full-site backups to a remote location (not your hosting account).

We recommend storing it on a cloud service like Amazon,

Dropbox, or private clouds like Stash.

Based on how frequently you update your website, the ideal setting might be either once a day or real-time backups.

Thankfully this can be easily done by using plugins like VaultPress or UpdraftPlus. They are both reliable and most importantly easy to use (no coding needed).

8.2.2 Best WordPress Security Plugin

After backups, the next thing we need to do is set up an auditing and monitoring system that keeps track of everything that happens on your website.

This includes file integrity monitoring, failed login attempts, malware scanning, etc.

Thankfully, this can be all taken care of by the best free WordPress security plugin, Sucuri Scanner.

You need to install and activate the free Sucuri Security plugin.

Upon activation, you need to go to the Sucuri menu in your WordPress admin. The first thing you will be asked to do is Generate a free API key. This enables audit logging, integrity checking, email alerts, and other important features.

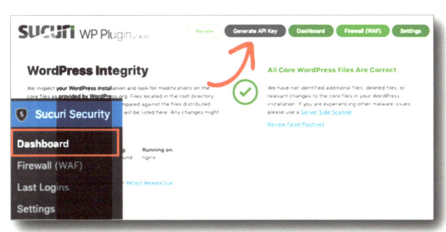

The next thing, you need to do is, click on the 'Hardening' tab from the settings menu. Go through every option and click on the "Apply Hardening" button.

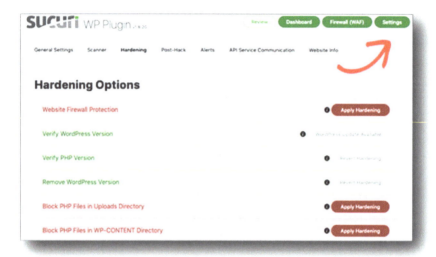

These options help you lock down the key areas that hackers often use in their attacks. The only thing we recommend customizing is 'Email Alerts'.

The default alert settings can clutter your inbox with emails. We recommend receiving alerts for key actions like changes in plugins, new user registration, etc. You can configure the alerts by going to Sucuri Settings » Alerts.

This WordPress security plugin is very powerful, so browse through all the tabs and settings to see all that it does such as Malware scanning, Audit logs, Failed Login Attempt tracking, etc.

8.2.3 Enable Web Application Firewall (WAF)

The easiest way to protect your site and be confident about your WordPress security is by using a web application firewall (WAF).

A website firewall blocks all malicious traffic before it even reaches your website.

DNS Level Website Firewall – These firewall route your website traffic through their cloud proxy servers. This allows them to only send genuine traffic to your web server.

Application Level Firewall – These firewall plugins examine the traffic once it reaches your server but before loading most WordPress scripts. This method is not as efficient as the DNS level firewall in reducing the server load.

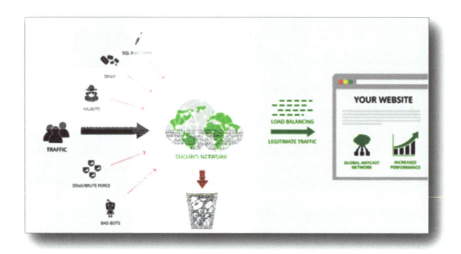

The best part about Sucuri's firewall is that it also comes with a malware cleanup and blacklist removal guarantee. Basically, if you were to be hacked under their watch, they guarantee that they will fix your website (no matter how many pages you have). This is a pretty strong warranty because repairing hacked websites is expensive.

8.2.4 Move Your WordPress Site to SSL/HTTPS

SSL (Secure Sockets Layer) is a protocol which encrypts data transfer between your website and a user's browser. This encryption makes it harder for someone to sniff around and steal information.

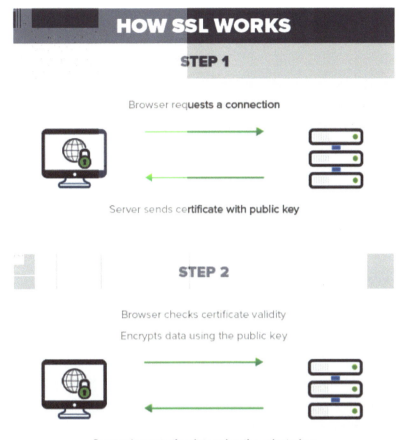

HOW SSL WORKS

STEP 1

Browser requests a connection

Server sends certificate with public key

STEP 2

Browser checks certificate validity

Encrypts data using the public key

Server decrypts the data using the private key

Once you enable SSL, your website will use HTTPS instead of HTTP, you will also see a padlock sign next to your website address in the browser.

SSL certificates were typically issued by certificate authorities, and their prices start from $80 to hundreds of dollars each year. Due to the added cost, most website owners opted to keep using the insecure protocol.

To fix this, a non-profit organization called Let's Encrypt decided to offer free SSL Certificates to website owners. Their project is supported by Google Chrome, Facebook, Mozilla, and many more companies.

Now, it is easier than ever to start using SSL for all your WordPress websites. Many hosting companies are now offering a free SSL certificate for your WordPress website.

If your hosting company does not offer one, then you can purchase one from Domain.com. They have the best and most reliable SSL deal in the market. It comes with a $10,000 security warranty and a Trust Logo security seal.

8.3 WordPress Security for DIY Users

If you do everything that we have mentioned thus far, then you're in pretty good shape. But as always, there's more that you can do to harden your WordPress security.

Some of these steps may require coding knowledge.

8.3.1 Change the Default "admin" username

In the old days, the default WordPress admin username was "admin". Since usernames make up half of the login credentials, this made it easier for hackers to do brute-force attacks.

Thankfully, WordPress has since changed this and now requires you to select a custom username at the time of installing WordPress.

However, some 1-click WordPress installers still set the default admin username to "admin". If you notice that to be the case, then it's probably a good idea to switch your web hosting.

Since WordPress doesn't allow you to change usernames by default, there are three methods you can use to change the username.

- Create a new admin username and delete the old one.
- Use the Username Changer plugin
- Update username from phpMyAdmin

Note: We're talking about the username called "admin", not the administrator role.

8.3.2 Disable File Editing

WordPress comes with a built-in code editor which allows you to edit your theme and plugin files right from your WordPress admin area. In the wrong hands, this feature can be a security risk which is why we recommend turning it off.

You can easily do this by adding the following code in your wp-config.php file.

```
1    // Disallow file edit
2    define( 'DISALLOW_FILE_EDIT', true );
```

Alternatively, you can do this with 1-click using the Hardening feature in the free Sucuri plugin that we mentioned above.

8.3.3 Disable PHP File Execution in Certain WordPress Directories

Another way to harden your WordPress security is by disabling PHP file execution in directories where it's not needed such as /wp-content/uploads/

You can do this by opening a text editor like Notepad and paste this code:

```
1    <Files *.php>
2    deny from all
3    </Files>
```

Next, you need to save this file as .htaccess and upload it to /wp-content/uploads/ folders on your website using an FTP client.

Alternatively, you can do this with 1-click using the Hardening feature in the free Sucuri plugin that we mentioned above.

8.3.4 Limit Login Attempts

By default, WordPress allows users to try to login as many times as they want. This leaves your WordPress site vulnerable to brute force attacks. Hackers try to crack passwords by trying to login with different combinations.

This can be easily fixed by limiting the failed login attempts a user can make. If you're using the web application firewall mentioned earlier, then this is automatically taken care of.

However, if you don't have the firewall setup, then proceed with the steps below.

First, you need to install and activate the Login LockDown plugin. For more details, see our step by step guide on how to install a WordPress plugin.

Upon activation, visit Settings » Login LockDown page to set up the plugin.

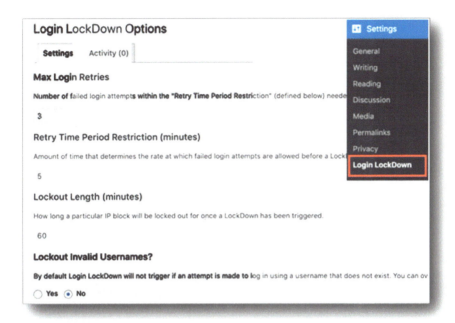

8.3.5 Add Two Factor Authentication

Two-factor authentication technique requires users to log in by using a two-step authentication method. The first one is the username and password, and the second step requires you to authenticate using a separate device or app.

Most top online websites like Google, Facebook, Twitter, allow you to enable it for your accounts. You can also add the same functionality to your WordPress site.

First, you need to install and activate the Two Factor Authentication plugin. Upon activation, you need to click on the 'Two Factor Auth' link in the WordPress admin sidebar.

Next, you need to install and open an authenticator app on your phone. There are several of them available like Google Authenticator, Authy, and Last Pass Authenticator.

We recommend using Last Pass Authenticator or Authy because they both allow you to back up your accounts to the cloud. This is very useful in case your phone is lost, reset, or you buy a new phone. All your account logins will be easily restored.

We will be using the Last Pass Authenticator for the tutorial. However, instructions are similar for all Auth apps. Open your authenticator app, and then click on the Add button.

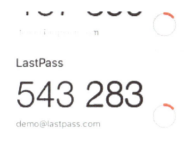

LastPass

543 283

demo@lastpass.com

You will be asked if you'd like to scan a site manually or scan the bar code. Select the scan bar code option and then point your phone's camera on the QRcode shown on the plugin's Settings page.

That's all; your authentication app will now save it. Next time you log in to your website, you will be asked for the two-factor auth-code after you enter your password.

Simply open the authenticator app on your phone and enter the code you see on it.

8.3.6 Change WordPress Database Prefix

By default, WordPress uses wp_ as the prefix for all tables in your WordPress database. If your WordPress site is using the default database prefix, then it makes it easier for hackers to guess what your table name is. This is why we recommend changing it.

Note: This can break your site if it's not done properly. Only proceed, if you feel comfortable with your coding skills.

8.3.7 Password Protect WordPress Admin and Login Page

Normally, hackers can request your wp-admin folder and login page without any restriction. This allows them to try their hacking tricks or run DDoS attacks.

You can add additional password protection on a server-side level, which will effectively block those requests.

8.3.8 Disable Directory Indexing and Browsing

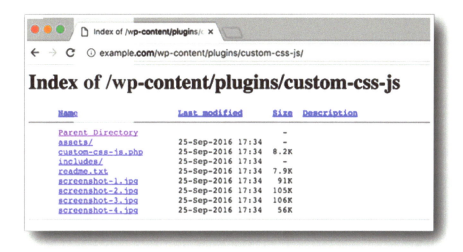

Directory browsing can be used by hackers to find out if you have any files with known vulnerabilities, so they can take advantage of these files to gain access.

Directory browsing can also be used by other people to look into your files, copy images, find out your directory structure, and other information. This is why it is highly recommended that you turn off directory indexing and browsing.

You need to connect to your website using FTP or cPanel's file manager. Next, locate the .htaccess file in your website's root directory. After that, you need to add the following line at the end of the .htaccess file:

Options –Indexes

Don't forget to save and upload .htaccess file back to your site.

8.3.9 Disable XML-RPC in WordPress

XML-RPC was enabled by default in WordPress 3.5 because it helps to connect your WordPress site with web and mobile apps.

Because of its powerful nature, XML-RPC can significantly amplify the brute-force attacks.

For example, traditionally if a hacker wanted to try 500 different passwords on your website, they would have to make 500 separate login attempts which will be caught and blocked by the login lockdown plugin.

But with XML-RPC, a hacker can use the system.multicall function to try thousands of password with say 20 or 50 requests.

This is why if you're not using XML-RPC, then we recommend that you disable it.

There are 3 ways to disable XML-RPC in WordPress, and we have covered all of them in our step by step tutorial on how to disable XML-RPC in WordPress.

Tip: The .htaccess method is the best one because it's the least resource-intensive.

If you're using the web-application firewall mentioned earlier, then this can be taken care of by the firewall.

8.3.10 automatically log out Idle Users in WordPress

Logged in users can sometimes wander away from the screen, and this poses a security risk. Someone can hijack their session, change passwords, or make changes to their account.

This is why many banking and financial sites automatically log out an inactive user. You can implement similar functionality on your WordPress site as well.

You will need to install and activate the Inactive Logout plugin. Upon activation, visit Settings » Inactive Logout page to configure plugin settings.

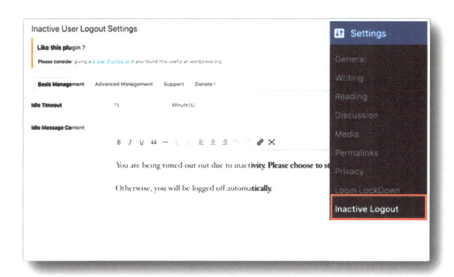

Simply set the time duration and add a logout message. Don't forget to click on the save changes button to store your settings.

8.3.11 Add Security Questions to WordPress Login Screen

Adding a security question to your WordPress login screen makes it even harder for someone to get unauthorized access.

You can add security questions by installing the WP Security Questions plugin. Upon activation, you need to visit the Settings » Security Questions page to configure the plugin settings.

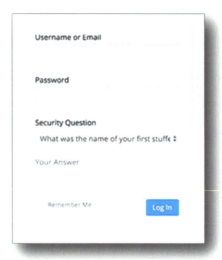

8.3.12 Scanning WordPress for Malware and Vulnerabilities

If you have a WordPress security plugin installed, then those plugins will routinely check for malware and signs of security breaches.

However, if you see a sudden drop in website traffic or search rankings, then you may want to manually run a scan. You can use your WordPress security plugin, or use malware and security scanners.

Running these online scans is quite straight forward, you just enter your website URLs and their crawlers go through your website to look for known malware and malicious code.

Now keep in mind that most WordPress security scanners can just scan your website. They cannot remove the malware or clean a hacked WordPress site.

This brings us to the next section, cleaning up malware and hacked WordPress sites.

8.3.13 Fixing a Hacked WordPress Site

Many WordPress users don't realize the importance of backups and website security until their website is hacked.

Cleaning up a WordPress site can be very difficult and time-consuming. Our first advice would be to let a professional take care of it.

Hackers install backdoors on affected sites, and if these backdoors are not fixed properly, then your website will likely get hacked again.

Allowing a professional security company like Sucuri to fix your website will ensure that your site is safe to use again. It will also protect you against any future attacks.

Conclusion:

As a site owner or developer, there will always be vulnerabilities and attack vectors to worry about but it's never been easier to maintain a secure WordPress install than it is today. The platform itself has been considerably hardened over the years and there are excellent plugin solutions to help you dial in your settings and sleep better at night.

Drag and drop WordPress website builder makes it easy for you to create and customize beautiful websites all on your own. We'll compare the most popular drag and drop WordPress page builders, so you can choose the best one for your needs and start creating your site.

Note: Instead of a WordPress page builder, if you're looking for a complete CMS/ website builder platform, then check out our collection of best website builders.

9.1 Why Use a Drag and Drop Page Builder for WordPress?

When starting a blog, many beginners find it difficult to customize their WordPress page layouts.

While a lot of premium WordPress themes come with different page layouts, most of them are extremely hard to customize for anyone who does not know code (HTML / CSS).

Well, there are several great drag and drop page builder plugins available for WordPress. They allow you to create completely custom website designs in WordPress without writing a single line of code.

Since there are so many different WordPress page builder plugins in the market, we decided to compare and rank the top WordPress page builders, so you can choose the right solution for your need.

Let's take a look at what you should keep in your mind when comparing the best WordPress page builders, so you can choose the right one for your needs.

- **Compatibility:**

If you're not interested in changing your existing WordPress theme for a page builder plugin, then the first thing you need to check is whether the builder you want to use is compatible with your WordPress theme.

If you find any compatibility issues, then you might want to use a builder-compatible theme for your site.

- **Features:**

You need to understand the unique quality of each builder when comparing the features. For example, some builders are shipped with a lot of built-in layouts while others offer dozens of animation effects.

- **Responsiveness:**

You need to make sure that the page builder you choose allows you to create responsive, mobile-friendly, layouts out of the box.

- **SEO:**

You need to make sure that your page builder is creating SEO friendly layouts.

Having said that, let's take a look at the best page builders for WordPress in the market.

1. **Beaver Builder:** Beaver Builder is a premium drag and drop page builder plugin for WordPress. It is by far the best WordPress page builder in the market.

   It is extremely fast and comes with a built-in onboarding tour to help you quickly familiarize with their interface.

   Beaver Builder comes with a live drag and drop interface. You get to see all your changes as you add them by simply dragging elements from the right sidebar and dropping them on your page. You can click on any element on a page to edit its properties.

There are modules that let you add almost everything you may want including sliders, carousel, backgrounds, content blocks, buttons, and more. It also comes with over 30 finely designed templates for landing pages that make it super-easy and super-fast to create stunning website layouts.

Beaver Builder has been updated well along with the Gutenberg project. So, it works fine with your new Gutenberg editor.

Pricing: Starting from $99 for Unlimited Sites.

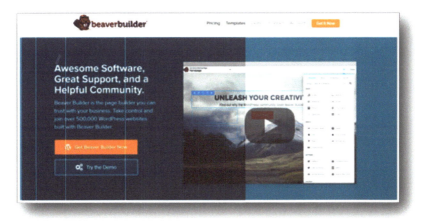

2. **The Divi Builder:** The Divi Builder is a powerful WordPress page builder that lets you build any type of design on your website with drag and drop. The Divi Builder is made by Elegant Themes, a renowned WordPress themes, and plugins company.

The Divi builder works on almost any WordPress website. It gives you endless possibilities to create the most advanced layouts without having to touch a single line of code.

The plugin is bundled with 46 builder modules, 20 row types, and 3 section types, all of which can be combined and arranged to create just about any type of website. With its advanced design settings, you can customize every element to a great extent.

That being said, if you want to make real-time changes on the design, then you might want to use the Divi theme. With the theme, you can build your page with the frontend editor, so your pages can be updated right from the frontend without having to switch back and forth from your dashboard to your website.

Pricing: Starts at $89 (includes 100+ website packs)

3. **Elementor:** Elementor is the first free and open-source advanced page builder for WordPress. With its quick drag and drop builder, you can make instant page edits from the frontend of your site. Elementor is well-known for its high-speed performance, which makes it fun and easy to build with.

With its extensive template library, you get hundreds of beautiful WordPress templates by their top-notch designers, which can be exported to different websites through the page builder. Elementor supports responsive mobile-friendly design, allowing you to build web pages that work great on any device.

Some other cool features of Elementor are:

- **Canvas:** You can build a brand new landing page without header or footer, optimized for high conversions.

- **Maintenance mode:** For maintenance, you can get your site offline with its built-in maintenance mode.
- **Zapier integration:** Integrating your website with a third-party web application is a breeze using its Zapier integration.

Pricing: Starts at $49 for a single site license.

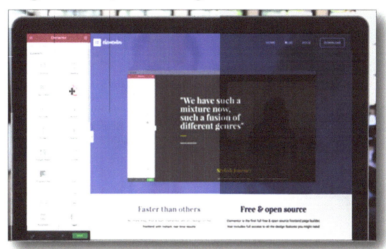

4. **Themify Builder:** The Themify Builder comes with a drag and drop interface that helps you create any layout you can imagine with ease. The builder comes with over 60 prebuilt layouts and animation effects that you can choose from. This means you can quickly build beautiful pages without having to start from scratch. All you have to do is simply import the layouts you want to use, replace the images and text, and you're done.

The builder comes as a standard feature for all Themify themes. You can also use their builder plugin with any third-party WordPress theme.

From the compact backend interface, you can use the drag and drop feature to build modules quickly and easily. In the frontend, you can preview the design and make live edits to your modules.

To enhance the capabilities of the Themify Builder, you can find tons of different add-ons which can be purchased separately or as a bundle.

Pricing: The core plugin is free. $39 for the addon bundle

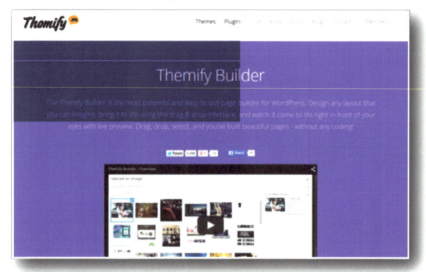

5. **Thrive Architect:** Thrive Architect is a page builder that's built for conversion-focused websites. Thrive Architect is developed by the same folks behind Thrive Themes, a company that sells conversion oriented WordPress themes and plugins.

Thrive Architect is shipped with a drag and drop editing tool and 271 prebuilt landing page templates. With Thrive Architect, you can quickly create a stunning homepage, sales page, blog posts, and everything you could ask for.

Pricing: Starts at $67 for a single site license or $19 per month for Thrive membership

6. **SiteOrigin:** SiteOrigin is one of the most popular WordPress page builders in the WordPress repository, with over a million active installs. With SiteOrigin, building a responsive, column-based content is a breeze. Your content will adapt to all devices, regardless of its screen resolution.

The SiteOrigin builder works seamlessly with your existing WordPress widgets, so you can add your favorite widgets to the websites you build. The builder works perfectly with any WordPress themes. The best part about SiteOrigin is that you can find a lot of neat compatible WordPress themes built by the same folks behind the SiteOrigin plugin.

The flexibility is one of the main benefits of the plugin. Using its advanced row builder, you can choose the exact number of rows for each column you add.

Pricing: Free

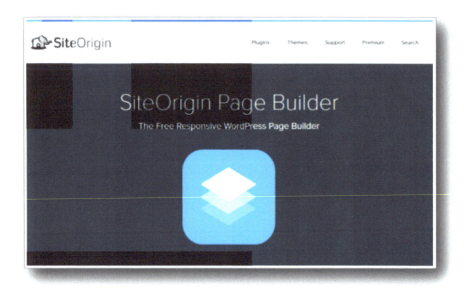

7. **WPBakery Page Builder for WordPress (formerly Visual Composer):** The WPBakery Page Builder for WordPress, formerly known as Visual Composer, is one of the most popular page builders in the CodeCanyon marketplace, a leading hub of premium WordPress plugins.

If you need a premium WordPress page builder that offers lifetime updates, look no further than WPBakery Page Builder. It comes with both frontend and backend editors, making content editing quick and easy.

The WPBakery Page Builder works seamlessly with popular WordPress plugins, including Yoast SEO and WooCommerce. It is also compatible with powerful translation plugins such as Polylang and WPML, so you can easily build multilingual websites powered by the builder.

Pricing: $46 for a single site license

Conclusion:

Almost every builder plugin out there comes with a drag and drop builder on the backend and a live editor on the frontend. It's important to understand what makes each WordPress page builder unique.

If you want to start a blog, then WordPress.com offers a hassle-free solution to get started. But the actual question is, what do you want to do with your Blog? A lot of people just want to share their personal thoughts, ramblings, photos and such. For that purpose, WordPress.com offers a free, easy to use, secure and stable platform for you to blog on. However, if you want to do more with your blog such as make money, build a membership community, among other things, then there are some inherent limitations. Let's take a look...

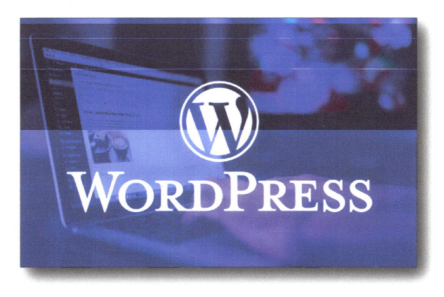

1. Earning Limitations

You cannot run Google AdSense or other advertising programs to serve ads on your WordPress.com blog. You cannot write paid posts, sell links, review products, etc. WordPress.com terms of service restrict you from using your free blog for any commercial activity on your own. However, you can apply for WordPress.com's advertising program which is called WordAds. This program is currently available to WordPress.com blogs that match certain traffic and quality requirements. Once you are approved for WordAds program, you will be sharing your advertising revenue with WordPress.com.

Note: If you have a book, then you can have an ad for that on your WordPress.com blog. They just don't allow ads for products or services that you do not own.

2. You Cannot Upload Plugins

The real power of WordPress comes from the freedom to customize and extend the core functionality. You cannot extend the functionality of WordPress.com by uploading plugins. You are given a comprehensive but still a limited set of features. A lot of people who migrate from WordPress.com to self-hosted WordPress.org do so just to take advantage of certain features that come with these amazing plugins.

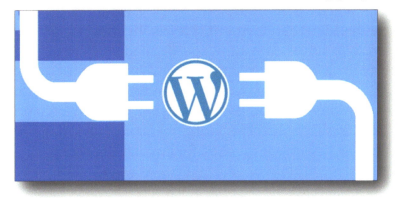

3. You Cannot Upload Themes

You can only use themes currently available to WordPress.com users. Some of these themes are free and others come with a one-time fee. In any case, the theme choice is very limited. Secondly, you cannot modify those themes. For an additional $30, you can add custom CSS and fonts to your theme but that is it. You cannot modify theme features or theme functionality. If you want to use one of the powerful eCommerce themes, or one of the many commercial themes that are not available to WordPress.com users, then you are out of luck. If you want to have a completely custom-built theme for you, then you are also out of luck.

4. Account Suspension

WordPress.com is very strict in protecting their services from abuse. They suspend blogs suspected of activities prohibited in their terms of service. Visitors can also report a blog. WordPress.com allows suspended blogs to export their posts for a limited time. Also, WordPress.com may not even notify or ask a blog owner to remove content. This means that usually there is no warning for the blog owner. Once a blog is suspended the WordPress.com subdomain will be held and will not be released for anyone else to use.

5. Not a Development Platform

WordPress has become a powerful content management system in itself. It is no more just a blog publishing platform. With WordPress.com, you are only getting a free blog service and not the actual powerful CMS features that are becoming the main reason for WordPress' popularity. To make it easier for you to understand is that let's suppose that you start with a basic blog and then want to offer online courses, sell digital downloads, or add a forum, or even an online store. It is not possible to do all this on your free WordPress.com blog.

Conclusion:

First of all, you need to realize what you want to do with your blog, make a plan and then choose. If you just need to express yourself then WordPress.com is an easy and wonderful option for you. But if you want to build on to your website and do more with your blog then consider WordPress.org.

When creating a WordPress website, everyone makes mistakes. However, each mistake is a learning opportunity that helps you grow. In setting up our own websites as well as helping others, there are some common WordPress mistakes to avoid to save time, money, and grow your business more effectively. The goal is to help you learn from other people's mistakes when making your own websites.

1. **Choosing The Wrong Platform:** The biggest mistake people make when starting out is choosing the wrong blogging platform. Basically, there are two types of WordPress. First, there is WordPress.com which is a blog hosting service, and then there is WordPress.org also which is the famous self-hosted WordPress platform that everyone loves.

You need to start with self-hosted WordPress.org because it gives you access to all the features you need out of the box.

2. **Buying More than What You Need:** To get started with a WordPress website, you need a domain name and WordPress hosting. The challenge is that a lot of domain registrars try to upsell other services. This confuses the small business owners who are just starting out.

The add-on services may include privacy protection, extra email accounts, security services, and more.

You can skip all of these things and save money to spend on growing your business. If you later decide that you need those services, then you can always purchase them from your hosting company.

You also need to choose the right hosting plan for your website. For 90% of websites that are just starting out, a shared hosting account is quite enough to get you going.

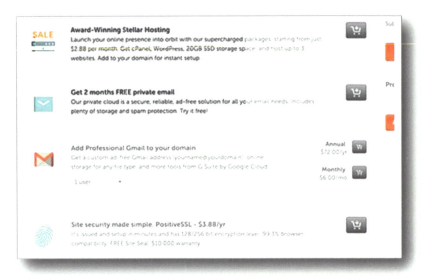

3. **Not Setting up Automated Backups:** Each year billions of dollars worth of damages are caused by data loss. Almost every website on the internet is prone to accidents, theft, hacking attempts, and other disasters.

Your most powerful line of defense against these threats is automated backups. Without a backup, you could lose all your WordPress data, and it would be very difficult to recover it (sometimes even impossible).

Setting up backups is extremely easy, and there are excellent WordPress backup plugins available in the market. Once you set up one of these backup plugins, they would automatically create backups for you.

The second part of this mistake is not storing backup files on a remote location. A lot of folks store their WordPress backups on their web hosting server. If they lose their website data, then they also lose the backups.

Make sure that you store your backups on cloud storage service like Google Drive, Dropbox, etc. Backup plugins like UpdraftPlus can automatically do that for you.

4. **Not Setting up Google Analytics:** If you want to grow your business with confidence, then you need to know how people find and use your website. That's where Google Analytics can help.

We recommend using MonsterInsights, the most popular Google Analytics plugin for WordPress. It saves you time during setup, and shows you the stats that matter, right inside your WordPress dashboard.

If you don't want MonsterInsights Pro, then there's also a free version of MonsterInsights available that you can get started with.

5. **Not Setting up a Contact Form:** Not setting up a contact form is another easily avoidable mistake that many beginners make. Without a contact form, your website visitors will not be able to contact you, and this can cause you to lose significant opportunities.

You will see a contact page on almost every popular website. It is one of the most important pages every website need to have.

WordPress does not come with a built-in contact form, but there are a lot of great WordPress contact form plugins available that you can use.

We recommend using WPForms Lite which is the free version of the popular WPForms plugin that's being used by over 2 million websites.

6. **Not Building an Email List:** Did you know that more than 70% of people who visit your website will never come back again?

If you are not building your email list, then you are basically losing money with every website visitor that leaves your site. Converting website visitors into email subscribers allows you to bring back those users to your website.

You will need an email marketing service to set up your email list. We recommend using Aweber because they are one of the best email marketing companies on the market with a very beginner-friendly platform.

7. **Not Choosing the Right WordPress Theme:** One of the biggest challenges WordPress beginners face is choosing the right design for their website.

With thousands of WordPress themes out there, an average beginner tries multiple themes before settling for the right one, and this process can even lead the user to rebuild their website multiple times.

To avoid this, we recommend choosing the right WordPress theme from the start and then stick to it.

This allows your website visitors to become familiar with your website, your brand, and its unique style. Consistency and continuity of your design make a big impact on brand recognition and awareness.

Well, when it comes to design we prefer simplicity over glitter. You need to choose a great looking but simple WordPress theme that pays attention to the following items:

- It must look equally good on all devices (desktop, mobile, and tablets).
- It should be easy to customize and flexible to adapt to your needs.
- It should work with popular plugins and WordPress page builders.
- It should be optimized for performance and speed.

Now we understand that as a non-techy user, you may not be able to check all those things on your own but do your best.

8. **Ignoring WordPress Updates:** Many beginners and even experienced WordPress users who don't install updates on their site. Many of them believe that doing so will cause errors and could break their site.

That's not true.

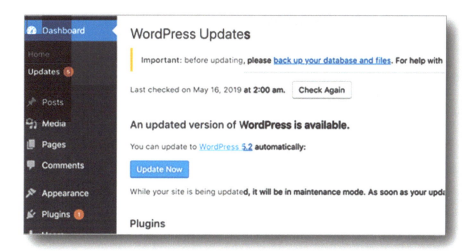

You can easily and safely update WordPress without breaking your website. By not updating WordPress, you leave your website vulnerable to security breaches while using outdated software.

It's not just WordPress, your WordPress theme and plugins also regularly release updates for bug fixes, security patches, and new features.

9. **Not Optimizing Your Website for SEO:** A lot of WordPress users rely on their best guesses when it comes to promoting their websites. Some completely ignore SEO, while some do it half-heartedly.

SEO (Search Engine Optimization) helps you rank higher in search engines, so more users can find your website.

Search engines are the biggest source of traffic for most websites. SEO is crucial for the success of your online business.

10.   **Not Using Categories and Tags Properly:** Another big mistake is not using categories and tags properly. Some users end up using categories where they should have used tags and vice-versa.

We have seen websites with dozens of categories and no tags at all. We have seen websites using hundreds of tags and no categories at all.

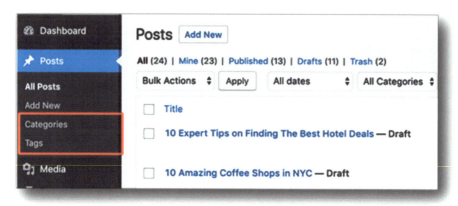

Basically, categories are your website's table of contents. If your website was a file cabinet, categories would be its drawers.

On the other hand, tags are like the index page. If your website was a file cabinet, tags would be the labels on individual file folders.

11. **Not Using Posts and Pages Properly:** Sometimes beginner WordPress users end up using posts to create important website pages. Similarly, some users end up using pages for articles when they should have used posts instead.

A lot of users realize their mistake after a while when their website becomes difficult to manage.

Basically, pages are for static pages that don't change very often like about, contact, privacy policy, etc.

On the other hand, posts are for time-based content like news, updates, articles, and blogs.

12. **Not Choosing The Right URL Structure (Permalinks):** Selecting the right URL settings (permalink structure) for your website is really important. Changing your URL structure later is not easy, and it can have a significant impact on your website traffic.

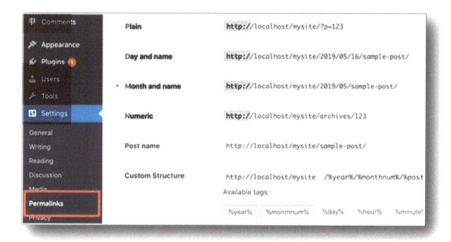

We recommend going to the Settings » Permalinks page in your WordPress admin area and choosing a URL structure with that shows your post name in the URL.

13. **Ignoring Website Speed and Performance:** Human attention span is dropping rapidly, and users want instant gratification. With faster internet connections, your users would find a few extra seconds of page load time to be extremely slow.

And it's not just users, even search engines rank faster websites higher in their results. By ignoring website speed and performance you risk user experience as well as search rankings.

Which is why you need to make sure that your website loads fast.

14. **Not Choosing The Right Plugins:** The real power of WordPress comes with its plugins. There are thousands of free WordPress plugins that you can install with a few clicks.

However, not all plugins are good. In fact, some plugins are bad and could affect your website's performance and security. Often users end up downloading plugins from unreliable sources that distribute hidden malware.

Here are a few things you need to keep in mind when

choosing plugins:

- Only install plugins from WordPress.org or WordPress companies with a good reputation.
- Look for plugin reviews and support forums because they are a good indicator of a plugin's quality
- Check trusted WordPress resources like WPBeginner for plugin recommendations

15. **Ignoring WordPress Security Best Practices:** Many users do not take any security measures to harden WordPress security. Some believe that their website is too small, and it will not be targeted by hackers.

Hackers target websites indiscriminately. For example, they could use your website to distribute malware, brute force attacks, steal data, and more.

By not securing your website, you can lose search rankings, your website data, and/or customer information. This could cost you a lot of money and headache.

You need to follow the security best practices and build layers of security around your WordPress site. It does not take too much time, and you don't need any special skills to do that.

16. **Changing Website URL and Losing All Traffic:** How many of you hated the first domain you registered and wanted to switch away from it when you got serious about blogging? Yup, it happens to all of us.

While you can change the website URL or domain name, it does have a significant SEO impact. What makes matters even worse is when you switch URLs without taking proper steps.

You need to set up proper redirects, inform Google about the change, and add the new domain to Google Search Console.

17. **Not Removing WordPress Demo Content:** A lot of people don't delete the default demo content added by a new WordPress install. This includes a sample page, a post titled 'Hello World', and a default comment.

New New Site — Just another WordPress site

Hello world!

Welcome to WordPress. This is your first post. Edit or delete it, then start writing!

Not removing this content allows search engines to crawl and index them. Now if you search for the text in demo content on Google, you'll find hundreds of thousands of pages. That's duplicate content and search engines penalize duplicate content as low-quality pages.

Similarly, many people don't change the default WordPress tag line that says 'Just another WordPress site'.

You need to delete all default content and the tag line, as they look unprofessional and create a bad impression.

18. **Not Setting up Comment Moderation:** Comment spam is annoying and can make your brand look bad. Many beginners have their blogs set up to automatically publish all new comments without moderation.

This means spam comments with links to malware and low-quality sites can go live on your website without your knowledge. This could damage your search rankings and your website's reputation.

You need to always keep comment moderation turned on for all your WordPress sites. Simply go to Settings » Discussion page and check the box next to 'A comment must be manually approved' option.

After that, you need to make it part of your routine to check and approve comments on your website.

19. **Not Optimizing Your Images for Web**: Images are essential in the making of a highly engaging website. However, they are also heavier in filesize than plain text.

If you are adding images to your website without optimizing them, then this would affect your website speed.

You need to make it a habit of saving your images as optimized for the web. You can use Photoshop, GIMP (free), or other online tools to reduce the image file size before uploading it.

20. **Saving Unnecessary Code in Theme's Functions File**: Another common mistake that we often come across is when folks add too many code snippets in their theme's functions.php file.

Functions file is designed to behave like a plugin, but it is not the ideal place for all types of code snippets. You will lose these modifications when you switch the theme. You may even forget that you added some code in there after a while. We recommend only adding code in your theme's functions file if the code is related to changing something with that particular theme.

21. **Getting Locked Out by Editing Functions File in WordPress Admin Area:** Another annoying mistake that is quite common is when folks edit functions file inside the WordPress admin area.

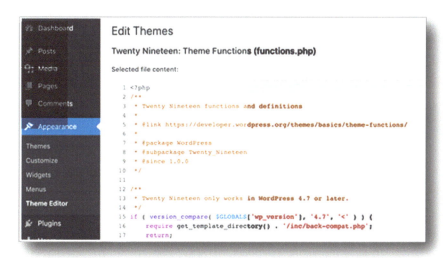

By default, WordPress comes with a built-in code editor to edit theme and plugin files inside WordPress. Often beginners end up breaking their website when adding or removing code using those editors.

Even though WordPress added functionality to catch fatal errors and not save them. You could still lock yourself out and make your website inaccessible.

22. **Not Setting Up Google Search Console:** Data is really important when planning a strategy to grow your business and website. Many users make the mistake of not adding their WordPress site to Google Search Console for a long time.

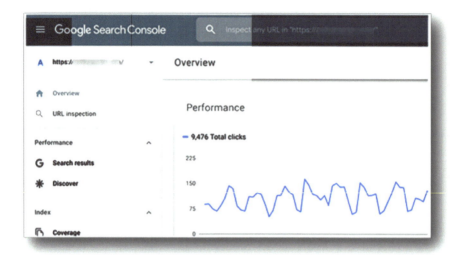

This means they miss out important search data that could help them grow their website.

Google Search Console is a free tool provided by Google. It allows you to see how your website appears in search results and fix any search indexing problems quickly.

23. **Using Uncategorized as Default Category:** A lot of folks leave Uncategorized as their default category. WordPress requires all posts to be filed under a category and when no category is selected, it automatically adds the post under default category.

Many times users forget to select a category for their post and hit the publish button which publishes that post in Uncategorized.

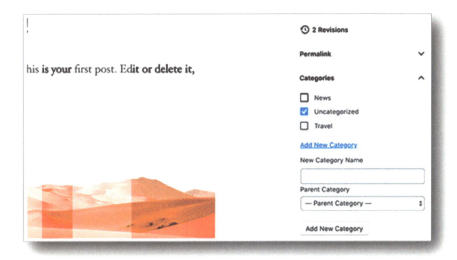

24. **Not Using a Professional Branded Email Address:** Many folks are sending emails from their Gmail or Hotmail accounts while pitching for a business that already has a website.

Now, how do we know for sure that they are officially representing that company or website?

Similarly, if you have a business, and you are still sending people business emails from a free email account, then people will have a hard time taking you seriously.

People do not have the time or skills to verify that you are the actual owner of that website or business.

25. **Leaving a Site Public While Working on It:** People often leave under construction websites publicly accessible. This is not very professional and can harm your business.

A publicly accessible website can be automatically crawled and indexed by search engines anytime. Your competitors can find it and steal your ideas. Your customers can find it and see the unfinished website.

There is an easier solution to avoid this mistake. Simply put your website in maintenance mode and add a coming soon page to build anticipation.

26. **Not Learning WordPress:** WordPress is very easy to use even for non-technical users. This allows many users to keep running their websites without learning more about WordPress.

By doing so, you miss the opportunity to explore the incredibly helpful features of WordPress. Things that are very simple to implement but could transform your business.

Learning WordPress is quite easy, particularly when you already have a running WordPress site. Explore different sections of WordPress, try out new plugins, learn more about SEO, and email marketing.

Conclusion:

Using WordPress to manage your website is a great idea. While WordPress can be a powerful tool, it's also a platform that's easy to make mistakes on, especially if you're a beginner. Don't fall victim to these common mistakes.

Having a great website matters. It's how you connect with your visitors and leads, create a positive first impression with new users, and boost conversions. The good news is creating your own website doesn't have to be a daunting process... At least not with WordPress.

The easy-to-use CMS offers completely customizable plans suitable for all needs. With no prior knowledge necessary, you can start building your own site for your business, blog, portfolio, or online store immediately.

WordPress is a very user-friendly and interactive way to host your website. And this 'WP Training Kit' training guide showed you how easy it is to install this CMS. One of the reasons why WordPress gained such massive popularity was its ability to customize and edit, as per the needs directly from the backend without hiring any professional or writing a single line of code.

But, that's not just about it, there's so much more. That being said, one thing is for sure - with a few tips and tricks, a lot can be done using WordPress. On the same lines, we hope that this 'WP Training Kit' training guide will help you in creating your WordPress website quickly and easily.

Enjoy Your Success!

www.ingramcontent.com/pod-product-compliance
Lightning Source LLC
Chambersburg PA
CBHW041151050326
40690CB00001B/437